Why It Works!

The Science Behind Manifesting Everything You Desire

By

Deborah Baker-Receniello, PhD, CLSC

First published by AuthorHouse 07/23/04

ISBN: 1-4184-5727-2 (e-book)
ISBN: 1-4184-4740-4 (Paperback)
ISBN: 1-4184-4741-2 (Dust Jacket)

Printed in the United States of America
Bloomington, Indiana

This book is printed on acid free paper.

1. Self Help/Transformation/Women's Issues
How To/Health Mind/Body/

DISCLAIMER

This book is designed to inform and educate the reader about the science behind getting everything you desire. This book is sold with the understanding that the publisher and author are not engaged in rendering medical advice or therapeutic remedies. If these services are required, the services of a competent professional should be sought.

The purpose of this book is not to include all references available to authors and/or publishers on this subject, but to support the premise that manifesting health, wealth, love and success are possible, given a new science paradigm. You are urged to read and educate yourself of all available material about the connection of mind, body, and spirit and tailor your own plan to your individual needs.

All case studies are factual, yet any name or reference to job title is fictitious due to confidentiality and protection to all.

CONTENTS

Part. I The Science

Part II. The Process

DEDICATION

This book is dedicated to my Beloved God and all the players on the stage of my life, whose interactions made me what I am.
Also to you, **each reader**, who are drawn to pick it up, read it and hopefully be inspired to continue your own journey to the extraordinary potential that you are.

ACKNOWLEDGMENTS

To my wonderful parents, **Douglas and Millie Baker** for the gift of LIFE, and to allow me the latitude to grow and explore my potentials in a safe environment.

To my beloved son, **Douglas Zukowski**, who keeps me aware of the child-like quality and curiosity I love so much.

To my beloved husband, **David Receniello**, for our incredible journey together, his dedication, support, encouragement, gifts of space to write, to be and love.

To my **Beloved God**, I owe all my experiences and wisdom.

As a Student of the Great Work, to my spiritual teacher, Ramtha for his Teachings and to J.Z.Knight for her tenancity and dedication.

To Life!

FORWARD

By: Howard F. Batie, Mh.D., and Director
Evergreen Healing Arts Center
Chehalis, Washington

The mind/body connection is both a mental concept and an energetic reality that deeply affects each of us in our own personal way; yet how this basic principle of life works has just recently begun to be understood. It affects how we feel about ourselves, how we interact with others, and determines to a surprisingly great degree our state of physical health and success in life.

Deborah Baker-Receniello, PhD and CLSC, has done a remarkable job of researching, integrating and making available a wide range of information across many disciplines and specialties. She describes in very understandable terms how this mind/body connection operates on not only the physical level of our being, but also on our emotional, mental and spiritual levels.

Scientists in many different disciplines have well-documented physical evidence that we humans are not just a mechanical-chemical composite. Instead, we are beings that can be fully appreciated and understood only if one takes into account our "wholistic" aspects that are usually lumped together and called the mind.

Dr Baker-Receniello is one uniquely qualified to approach this task in codifying these new findings and to present them in a comfortable, easy to comprehend presentation. She easily connects the scientific field of cellular biology, chemistry and quantum physics and also incorporates a well-rounded understanding of philosophy, attitudes, feelings and spirituality in her discussion.

In her book, you will be led on an exciting and enlightening journey to understand connection between the mind and the body, the mental processes of thinking, the kinesthetic feelings of emotions and attitudes, the recent scientific breakthroughs in areas of physics, biology and physiology, and how all these disciplines synergistically function to determine one's state of physical, emotional, mental and spiritual well-being.

The late Reverend Paul Solomon said, "We are all child gods, growing up to be like our father". As we awaken to our natural talents and abilities and grow to appreciate our individual and collective roles as cosmic citizens of this universe, we will be called upon to accept the greater responsibility to ourselves and to others that accompanies this new wisdom. It is time to let go of our perceived limitations, the comfortable boxes we have lived in, our beliefs in a thousand reasons why something can not be done, and to acknowledge that whatever we believe we are, we become; whatever we believe we do, and we make it happen.

Dr. Baker-Receniello deserves great credit for bringing her inspirational message to all of us in a clear and understandable manner, and for urging each of us to begin taking our next evolutionary steps, one person at a time, toward a grander vision and appreciation of who we are and of what we are naturally capable.

Howard F. Batie, Mh.D., Director
Evergreen Healing Arts Center—
Chehalis, Washington

INTRODUCTION

The Journey Begins...

Each of us creates every moment of our entire life by sending out thoughts, feelings, emotions, or declarations into a quantum void, in the form of energy frequency that weaves the universe. The secret—every quantum physicist will tell you nothing exists in the universe except as possibility. We continually co-create by remaking everything real and touchable.

The search for personal identity comes from a desire to know who are we, really? Are we more than our physical bodies? What are we capable? Why are we here? Is there more to life than being a success at work or having a family? Is there more than survival? How many times have we looked to the physical world to define us or give us answers to these questions?

Perhaps we need to look beyond the surface or visible world for answers to these questions. To begin to understand the immensity of what we are, we can engage in the study of biology, genetics, brain functions, physics, philosophy, and psychology along with our inner, unique workings of mental, emotional, and spiritual experiences. This may be an internal study, private, and often times a mystery.

While attending a lecture on the use of Hypnotherapy in multiple personalities back in the seventies, I had the opportunity to meet the "infamous" Eve. The book and subsequent movie *Three Faces of Eve* were based on her life; she astoundingly had as many as 24 personalities. That in it's self was quite unbearable to her. One personality had severe, crippling arthritis, one wore bottle-thick glasses, and one played the piano and one a creative artist. The "Strawberry Lady" would eat strawberries—she loved pink and would decorate an entire room in pink. Another personality hated strawberries and was allergic to them.

The gist of the lecture was devoted to the therapist's use of hypnosis to integrate these personalities. A fascinating fact about this saga is how each personality portrayed distinct and different behaviors to a point where the biology of her physical presence would change with each transformation. Read this again. Videos demonstrated each personality with certain behavioral and biological differences displayed, only moments apart, changed. Here, my quest began to understand what can manifest these differences, so clearly, and so rapidly in the same body—and if understood, produce healing in any body.

In my hypnotherapy practice, some patients would show remarkable strides: reducing tumors, recovering from strokes and heart attacks—living well beyond the prediction that they would die in a few months, to regenerating use of their body when it was practically destroyed beyond hope? These questions, and others, sparked a life-long journey to gain knowledge and understanding of the mind/body/spirit connection.

The medical profession considered for a long time that the mind and body were separate, functioned independently, and should be treated as such. Descartes, 17th century French mathematician and philosopher enshrined this metaphysical divide in what is known today in Western Philosophy as mind/body dualism.

The belief, that the body was sophisticated and driven by machine-like programming lead to the belief that illness was an invasion to the natural system from an outside force. This thinking resulted in the treatment of disease, and as such, had no room for spontaneous healing. Techniques for curing the body or maintaining health and vitality using the power of the mind were not considered.

Eastern mystical traditions concluded the opposite. The Mind and Body belong to an indivisible continuum. When we re-examine, however, the definition of quantum theory, body, brain, emotion, mind, consciousness, love, and the relationship of all of these—we may have a different picture. Hang in here now; let's investigate this new paradigm.

What powers exist in a healer's touch? How do the masters of the Far East control breathing, heartbeat, and skin temperature? Spontaneous regression? How can tumors disappear overnight? Do I have any control?

Can anyone learn to harness this phenomenon for our own benefit? We are learning to manage stress, but can the mind somehow transform a crippled, arthritic person to a supple, nimble musician in a moment? Can a person injured in a bicycling accident—sustained while traveling at 45 mph and suddenly falling on gravel, impacting the knee, tearing cartilage, dislocating bone, damaging connective tissue—walk normally in 7 days?

Manifesting, is defined by Webster as:

"The act or process of instance of manifesting. Manifest easily understood by the mind; readily perceived by the senses; a future event accepted as inevitable." The last one is the one I love most. You have the power to put forth into your life whatever you choose with purpose. To manifest is to bring into materialism. Materialism to make material; that which is perceived by the senses, understood by the mind and a future experience accepted as inevitable.

Why is it that sometimes visualization, affirmations creative visualization, see it, do it and be it, act as if, sometimes do not work? In this book we will look at these questions and understand these powerful, even life-changing techniques.

This book is divided into two parts: The Science behind getting what you desire and the manifestation process. You will be shown how to create everything you desire. This book is set up with the **process** of manifestation (making material your dreams and desires) last because before we can begin DOING... you must begin with IDENTIFYING WHO WE ARE REALLY, what's the beginning of ALL BEINGNESS, followed by RIGHT USE OF THINKING AND FEELING, then DEFINING WORDS and IMAGINATION and finally with ACTION.

You will discover what each of us is made of, clearly showing a brief explanation of Quantum Physics, Mind, Brain Functions, Body, Emotions, Beliefs, and Imagination; and bring all these pieces of the puzzle together so a whole new picture emerges of what most may consider *impossible* or as I have learned, *a miracle is just commonplace*. You will discover that mind and body, spirit and matter are not separate things after all.

Take the time to read and understand the science, you will be glad you did. You can apply it to the process. It's about going way beyond what's now being called virtual reality. It's about totally immersing yourself in any adventure, any character or any kind of experience that interests you. It's about creating the most exciting vision you can possibly create and start living that vision by absolute design.

It is in your grasp to be the President of the United States, the Super Bowl winning quarterback, a gold medal winning athlete, a billionaire, a spy behind enemy lines, a musician, a great parent, a general leading an army into battle or corporate coop, a spiritual leader, a researcher, painter, acing that test, master any craft or a loving person—anything that you could possibly imagine.

When you hear that you are capable of anything, just have faith, believe, all your riches are at your feet—wouldn't you be more likely to believe when you know the science behind these statements?

Let's look at the definitions more closely and re-examine them using the theories of quantum physics, biology, chemistry, physiology, psychology and philosophy. Perhaps you can find the key to unlock the door all our dreams, whether it be health, wealth, love, genius, wisdom, or fulfillment.

There is a caveat to this experience; the awareness alone is not as important as the necessity to bring that awareness into play in your everyday life. The value of the new science is in reprogramming limiting perceptions (beliefs) we have acquired, for they are the primary roadblocks to our success.

The quantum is both readily accessible and mysterious. To experience it we have only to turn our attention to the subatomic world; but in trying to explain it to others, we immediately encounter a problem; the language evolved for the most part to deal with aspects of the outer rather than the inner world.

Let's begin this journey with understanding just what is the human body.

Chapter 1

Defining Human Body

Sometimes we need to relearn what we know
To learn what we do not know, so we can
Know. Author Unknown

The Sanskrit word meaning "the science of life" is Ayurveda. The human body is defined as a fluctuation of energy and information in a larger field of energy and information, the void or God. The quantum mind/body is thought and feeling, desire, impulses of intelligence and information. The body is not so much a 'thing' as it is a process. Therefore, the process, which comprises the body are functions that shift, change and flow.

Ask a physicist, what is the essential nature of the basic unit of matter that makes up flesh and bones? You could learn that an atom is made up of sub-atomic particles, which are not really material objects, but rather they are fluctuations of energy and information in a void of energy and information. **The essential raw material of the body turns out to be non-material.** If you looked at it, you would see a huge void with a few scattered dots and spots and some random electrical discharges. Although empty space, it is intelligence. That non-material quality of information (thought) and energy that regulates, constructs, and governs; actually becomes the body physical.

Max Planck, Nobel Prize-winning father of quantum theory once stated that **there is no matter as such! All matter originates and exists only by virtue of a force. We must assume behind this force the existence of a conscious and intelligent** MIND. This **MIND is the matrix of all matter.**

Our bodies are a collection of billions of sub-atomic and atomic particles forming cells which collectively form tissue, which form organs, then systems, and all are surrounded by water and mostly space. This "mostly space" is pure potentiality; energy and information. A physicist will tell you that an atom is 99.999% empty space; a nucleus with circling particles that are not material but energy and information. The quantum light is a photon, the quantum gravity is a graviton, and the quantum electricity is an electron.

Webster states that the body is defined as:
a. the entire material or physical structure of an organism, especially of a human being or an animal. b. The physical part of a person. c. A corpse or carcass.

The human body is like a complex organization that has an important job to get done on a tight deadline. In order to get everything done perfectly and on time, it has to use a system. Actually, the human body uses many systems that work side by side.

The real self, being information and energy, interacts with our own self-consciousness and becomes a mind/body. The body is then like a river. The banks may remain relatively stable, yet the water flowing through is ever changing. The very air you breathe in your lungs is exhaled and shared with all others, and vice versa. You are literally sharing atoms with Christ, Leonardo DaVinci, Khan, Einstein, Deborah, Joe and Shirley.

The physical body is a body of consciousness (thought), say constructed in 1950, sleek, young, intelligent, compassionate, supple machine, with special interests. Yet, the 2003 model is not the same. It is under constant, ever-present construction.

The brain acts as a receiver and transmitter. Receiving stimuli from our senses electrically, the brain transmits these stimuli along neurological passageways, translating chemical and hormonal actions. This signals the central nervous system causing the organs, tissues, and muscles into some form of reaction.

Science now tells us that thought in the brain creates chemical messengers called neuropeptides that communicate with other brain cells. The brain cells have receptors that collect the information of the neuropeptides. Science has also discovered that other cells have receptors, including

3

immune T-cell, etc. that ease-drop on the communications from the brain. That makes **cells, conscious beings having information and energy**. So, mind is not confined in the brain, but in every cell of the body or anything.

It would therefore appear that the body has no definite beginning in time and space and it is not moving toward some predetermined end. The physiology is constantly remaking itself every second and will continue to do so as long as it exists. If this is done properly, can we live to be 200 years old? Exactly, how it continues to do so can be directly influenced by signals your brain sends in regard to everything you do: your job, relationships and certainly what you think, how you feel and what you eat. If you continue to replay the same negative thoughts and feelings that have burdened you for many years, you will continue to have the same physiology. Fortunately, you can change all that. Let's take a deeper look at how quantum physics, energy and intelligence work.

Chapter 2

The Quantum World-Web of Energy and Intelligence

Knowing what you and the world are made
Of is the first key to knowing how to make
Your reality what you desire…author

In the following chapters, you will learn dramatic and undeniable evidence of a newly discovered form of energy, a matrix, or blueprint linking each of us, creation and the events of our lives in unexpected and enabling ways. You will be challenged to look at your true identity. Not the person you have created by what you believed you are supposed to be or told to be. It is the person you have always wanted to be, but, were too afraid, busy, or distracted to be.

Up to now, some of this information was found in technical journals and received little attention from our media, yet can shake the foundation of our predominant worldview.

If you are to be the *architect of your new design, you must understand the blueprint and how it works.* Quantum physics helps us understand how the physical matter comes about and our role in it. This knowledge explains how our beliefs and thinking creates matter and how we all reap what we sow.

Quantum Physics is a branch of science that deals with subatomic indivisible units of energy called quanta that scientifically documents:

1) The view of the world is a vast oscillation of interconnected forces; a web of life.
2) We communicate with our world in an unrecognized form of energy that operates outside the bounds of measured time and space; non-physical and non-local.
3) Our DNA is directly influenced by our physical world (our environment, thoughts, beliefs and emotion) through this energy.
4) Energy is not continuous, but comes in small discrete Units called quanta, flashing randomly and rapidly.
5) Quantum packets have intelligence and can make decisions.
6) Quanta respond to the observer.
7) Quanta are defined as probabilities of existence and are multidimensional.
8) Elementary particles behave both like particles and like waves.
9) It is physically impossible to know both the position and momentum of a particle at the same time. The more precisely one is known, the less precise the measurement of the other is.

10) The atomic world is nothing like the physical world we live in.

No solid object is really solid. It's made of rapidly flashing packets of energy. They are very tiny in the subatomic realm, billions and even trillions of packets of energy.

With this information, you begin to see that you can change your view of reality. With your new perception, you can change your creation of reality; first stage to manifesting your dreams.

Your mind interacting, with quantum, keeps your body solid. Your mind does the same with other things around you. All matter is put together using information from your mind and the minds of those around you and the rest of the universe.

Energy and Matter are connected and are quantum possibilities awaiting an observer, for its experiences. In quantum mechanics, the observer and that which is being observed become linked so that the results of any observation seemed to be determined in part by actual choices made by the observer. In the manifestation process, it's important to know your thoughts and make them very clear with your intent and without judgments or negative emotion. Thought can collapse the wave function (energy) into particles (separate possibilities) simultaneously. Quanta can be physical particles and, at the same time a wave, carrying information.

The quantum world is real. The world you see with you eyes is a perception of a group of quantum activity, which is caused by you. Erwin Schrodinger, who was awarded the Nobel Prize in 1933, did an amazing experiment, called "Schrodinger's Cat" Experiment. He concluded that everything exists in all possible states until you observe it. (Appendix 2)

When the electron is observed, it is forced to choose one path. Neils Bohr called this the 'collapse of the wave function'. Bohr reasoned **that nature likes to keep its possibilities open, and follows every possible path. Only when observed is nature forced to choose only one path, so only then, is just one path taken.** Here's real power for manifestation. With focused intention and will, you the observer, collapse the quantum possibilities to the dream you hold in mind. That's power.

Einstein stated **that the only reality is that of energy organized into fields.** If all matter were disintegrated, we would be left with a field, the primary source, the Void, Mind of God or Quantum Foam. The Human mind can be seen as the mind-field. The characteristics of body tissue and the nature of transactions with outside fields determine its dynamic, non-random organization, which fits the classical mathematical chaos pattern. The mind-field (quantum) is the first contact with the primary world. It is composed of both alternating and magnetic currents of electromagnetic spectrum. We may speculate the more fluid the field, the more interaction with other fields.

Karl Pribram, the Nobel Prize winner for his brain hologram research, **commented that the holographic images that we see are existing in the mind somewhat outside of the brain machine that produces these—as though the mind hovers like a protective entity beyond the brain's machinery. The Quantum!** (Appendix 3)

Dr. Robert Becker, an Orthopedic Surgeon, conducted research into bioelectrical properties of the body and published his results in the book, *The Body Electric.* Dr. Becker's interest was in regeneration. He concluded that **the secret lies in the unifying bio-field properties of the body, the quantum, as we know today.**

Dr. Larry Dossey stated, **eventually our concepts of how our bodies work will have to give due regard to quantum physical events and the...subatomic world.**

We are an open system in which reality is tremendously complex. Intuition and consciousness operate interdependently with matter and transform matter as they are transformed by it.

Our bodies are made of systems, that are made of organs, that are made of cells, that are made of molecules that are made of atoms, which in turn, are made of sub-atomic particles such as electrons, protons, and neutrons—the basic building blocks of our known universe.

Use of the word, particle, is not the same definition as a particle of sand. Sand is at the atomic level. Remember, the sub-atomic particles are not objects; they are probabilities of existence and at the same time, multiple existences. The famous split screen experiment demonstrates this. (See Appendix 1)

Everything interpenetrates everything, and although human nature may seek to categorize and pigeonhole and subdivide, the various phenomena of the universe, all apportionments are of necessity artificial and all of nature is ultimately a seamless web.

The electrons in a carbon atom in the human brain are connected to the subatomic particles that comprise every salmon that swims, every heart that beats, every drop of water, each ray of light, and every star that shimmers in the sky.

When we go back to the body and ask what's it made of, we journeyed from systems to the sub-atomic world. What is sub-atomic world made of? Most answer energy. The fact is the subatomic world is not made of energy—it **IS** energy. Everything is made of energy. Erwin Schrodinger created quantum equations based on wave mathematics. He stated that the **atomic world is nothing like our world, no matter how much we try to pretend it is.**

Medical diagnosis is based on description and classification of symptoms and pathological states, the mind and emotions have been given less recognition. Electro-medical researchers believe that each disease of functional disturbance has its own energy field, which must be reversed before healing can take place.

Illness is a disturbance first in the energy field and healing is the restoration of that field to health. Emotions disturb the field to distort or enhance something other than its harmonic state. Thoughts create emotions. Shamans, Spiritual, and Psychic healers place primary emphasis upon healing the soul when it gets off track. They believe that the source of all illness is forgetting who we are, the observer.

The quantum void is not empty space devoid of anything. It supposes the existence of a field, yet undetectable. We can see its effects, because it links real particles to one another and seems agitated to us, but we cannot see it. We call it empty while it is full - full of potentials of all matter. Leading physicists conclude that this invisible sub atomic quantum field is the ground state of the universe. What if the Mind of God, the void, Quantum, or nature are names used for the same mind field that is composed of intelligence and energy? Consciousness or intelligence and energy is birthed from the void where all potentials reside. God, the void, Quantum, or nature is the collective mind of all that has lived, will live and lives now, all powerful, and all places at the same time. (omnipresent, omnipotent, omniscient).

Physicists say the quantum has the ability to make decisions, powered by intelligence, and can instantaneously transverse space and time. This quantum is not solid, so particle X can get to particle Z without having to cross the space in between, even, if Z and X are at different times. Think about this. Now you can see that you, by observation and collapsing the waveform, become the controller. Now you can see the importance of choosing your thought, beliefs, attitudes, and what you want to see.

This quantum is also multidimensional. Your senses can detect length, width, height and time; this is only using 10% of your brain. When you open your brain to more potential we then can perceive more. The Quantum is made of a mirage of energy packets that are not bound by space and time, has no boundaries. Your mind is connected to this universal mind, quanta, Mind of God and becomes one mind. You are more than you once thought.

Here is a diagram to help demonstrate this concept. Below is a blank space, which represents the Mind of God, the Void, the ultimate ground of all Being-ness, Spirit, or quantum. Now, this blank space does not mean that it is featureless nothingness—it is a representation of the tract that it is non-conceptual, non-dual, non-objective, no time, yet holds the potential of everything—a seething cauldron of all potential. Stretch your imagination, because this space has no limits, no boundaries no lines; looks like empty space, just is chuck full of potentials:
The Quantum void:

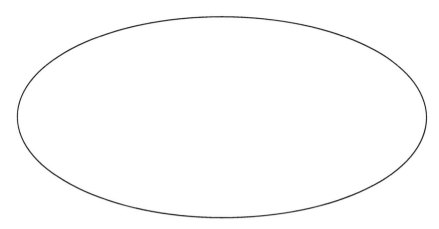

Now, if you impress this Mind of God, Void or quantum foam with individual minds (people), concepts (beliefs), duality, objectivity (things), a dream (goal), and time, let's see what happens upon slicing a tiny square out and overlay it, as follows:

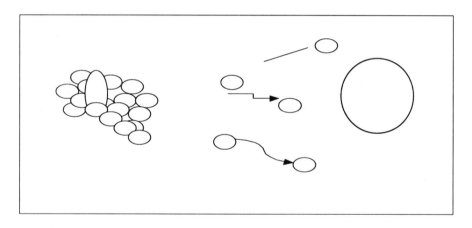

Here, you have cut a section of the Mind of God, Void, or Quantum and created a personal mind; and through that mind have thought create individuals concepts, dreams, duality and time. Therefore creating a reality. Yet, beyond this personal mind, the greater mind (quantum, void or Mind of God) still exists around this sliced rectangle.

It all begins to look like a cosmic soup. Quantum physics says everything is made up of energy and exchanges that energy with everything else at all times in a most complex way. Energy is the building block of all matter. The same stuff that makes your flesh is the same that makes the stone on your home, the flowers, the animals, birds, etc.

Everything about you ripples out into this soup. Everything else ripples in and gives you feedback. As without, so within or as above, so below, begins to sound familiar. Your thoughts ripple out and your experiences are a rippling reflection of those thoughts back to you.

Existing in this quantum, Mind of God, is the potential for everything. You can literally be and do anything. The doing is the trick. An example, you can drive a car. You make the decision to do so. You need to educate yourself on how to, then, have the experience of driving. You have the ability for anything. You just need to prepare yourself for the experience. To prepare is to make you consciously aware of the possibility and embrace the experience.

Now is the time to become the explorer in this vast ocean or cosmic soup of potentiality. Eastern philosophies present ideas and exercises supposedly to clarify the mind or sharpen it. What if these techniques in fact, subtly reorganize the field, which in turn mechanically changes the brain? Many of us believe that when enough minds focused together, we could stop floods, hurricanes, tornadoes and even earthquakes. Healing groups. We could create peace. There have been some organized groups believe the focused mind-field has the power to tap into everything going on in the world. This may explain telepathy, healing at a distance, etc.

It begins to look as though energy field patterns are related to streams of consciousness or awareness—a function of the mind. When your personal field reaches higher vibrational states, you no longer experiences materials things in the same way. You experience knowingness, higher information, transcendental ideas, insight about sources of reality and creativity in its pure form, time distortion, and miracles.

Isn't it interesting that you can believe that you can send and receive radio signals, bounce them off satellites, unscramble them and have information transmitted over a distance and you cannot accept that all the marvelous things we invent or discover "out there" or really prototypes of the body, brain, and it's mind. Most try and are surprised when this works. **Should you be?**

Let's see what consciousness has to do with.

Chapter 3

Consciousness & Mind

*Our normal waking consciousness, rational
consciousness as we call it, is but one
special type of consciousness, whilst all
about it, parted from it by the filmiest of
screens, there lie potential forms of
consciousness entirely different.*
                    William James, Psychologist

*As long as man derives sensations from a
contact with nature, he is her slave; but as
soon as he begins to reflect upon her
objects and laws he becomes her lawgiver.*
Letters upon the Æsthetic Education of Man
                    J. C. Friedrich von Schiller

Physical theory is not complete until
consciousness is acknowledged as an active
element in the establishment of reality. This
seems to present a dilemma, consciousness does
not fit into the time, space and mass
constructs of material physics.

Consciousness, as focused intention or will,
is the precursor of all material things.

Energy, as an electromagnetic current, is the active ingredient that jiggles the quantum soup to create your desire.

Thought, as consciousness, encompasses a full spectrum of electromagnetic radiation and ranges from the finest and the most penetrating cosmic rays to the densest and least energetic radio waves. It is described as being composed of several shades or levels—although these levels are not separate layers, but rather mutually penetrating forms of energy from the finest down to the densest form of "materialized thought" (matter). In other words, conscious awareness as an intelligence living in an atmosphere incorporates thoughts, beliefs, emotions, limitations and desires to influence matter. You and your desire are not separate things. Your atmosphere of thought, emotion, beliefs, limitations and desires **is** the energy that will move the conscious thought or focused intention into your material world. You may look relatively the same each day, yet you are really a body of fluctuating energy.

Remember the comic strip character that was a little boy that has an aura or atmosphere of dirt that surround him everywhere he went. He drops some and picks some up as he interacts with his world. Your desire may be fragmented if your atmosphere is fragmented. If you desire a loving relationship, yet, do not trust men; you will attract a relationship where trust is an issue. If you desire more money, yet believe money is the root of evil; you will attract the evils of money. If you desire a new automobile, yet, do not feel worthy; you may attract an accident and

17

through that accident a newer automobile with the unworthy physical effects. If your intention is clear, concise, and filled with passion, your desire will manifest as such.

Consciousness then, is understood better through a synthesis of the information gained on each level; as a subtle field of components with organized energy patterns, boundaries and definitions, and that atmosphere governs the laws of existence.

Your intent converts matter as waves collapsed into particles within the possibility—every event of perception, observation, and experience. Our brain is a micro-bio-computer, which allows where you put attention to choose that potential to pursue. Everything is a consciousness, which then gives order to chaos in the world of matter.

The power of the Mind of God or Quantum Void is an intelligence and energy, not energy in the form of electricity or fossil fuels, but a vital current of electromagnetic energy, prana, or chi.

Here's a simple exercise looking at atmosphere and dimensionality. Look at an object say a rose then look again. Seeing it differently each time will demonstrate the indivisibility of the spectrum or atmosphere. Imagine a rose.

Your first thought may picture it to be red, yellow, or pink.

Look closer. See the petals, stem, and leaves, perhaps stamen, pollen, interaction with the bees and its environment.

It is subtle and there is a whole science of interaction. Inside you begin to see how it takes in light, water and minerals. Look at it again, see where it came from—the rose bush. See again, the thought of the one who planted the bush, with their love of its perfect perfume exuded just before dusk.

Perhaps see the owner's interactions with beauty, placement, serenity or joy. See the human with her adventurous thoughts and where these thoughts originated. Perhaps she originated from the South. The sheer romance of the rose conjures many illusions.

Then again, you can trace the rose all the way back to the great silence or void, which contains all things "potentially." Can you see it is the thought of the rose that begins its process to materialization? The rose cannot be divided itself, but, as a thought gathering potential particles to form it into its totality. The consciousness is information that is held in the form of a rose.

The fun is recognizing the science, adventure and romance of your dreams and desires connected to the whole of life.

The idea that the mind is unique from the brain and it has its own self-consciousness, which monitors awareness outside the realm of material reality, intrigues me. The idea that the mind experiences non-physical reality leads to the thought of the mind as an all encompassing field, often referred to Mind of God, Void or quantum.

Personal Mind is the result of consciousness, as thought or intelligence, imprinted upon your brain, experienced through your body and accepted as your truth or reality. Personal Mind is the collective storehouse of experiences, education, laws, beliefs, habits and truths that are accepted by you. Personal mind also has a spectrum, for example, each person's mind is a collective storehouse and the mind of every other individual with their collective storehouse within the Greater Mind.

Therefore it is easy to understand the term—mind-set, or having the mind set to do something—a focused, concentrated effort of thought to a directed end. Or half a mind! This is important in the manifestation process. You can only manifest equal to your consciousness awareness be it limited or expanded.

It also explains how a personality can completely change and have different physiology with it, remember Eve.

All of the body including the brain is in the mind—yet, not all-of-the mind, is within the body. If you were to ask the question, who am I? One answer may involve only externals: I am a woman, 50 years old, born in New Orleans, educated, creative, innovative, married with one son, Personal Coach, Author, and Trainer. These are all qualities, which are the results of specific events, people, time, places and things that pertain to me. They are labels that identify.

Yet, more profound, these do not define you at all. No one can define you with any attachment, not the inner essence, free will, silent observer, infinite potential, unlimited spirit. That "inner you" is beyond boundary, and unseen; yet felt. It cannot be explained in a rational, linear, cause-and-effect mind.

Do you identify with, I am a physical body (outer self or personal mind) or I am all encompassing spirit, express through a physical body (inner self or greater mind). If, I am a body, then I shift from the identity of wholeness to an altered ego, separated and fragmented. Therefore, my manifestations, dreams, and desires may be fragmented.

Personal or self-consciousness then goes about altering that ego by refusing to admit unwanted aspects of self. This identity then shifts to fragments or shadow selves. Shadows are the judgments, beliefs, limitations, and untested acceptance of other's beliefs. All these are functions of conscious thought. If, I am inner essence, I have a body to express through.

The mind is an all-inclusive entity to itself—non-dual in the timeless ground of all temporal phenomena. You have reality without duality, but not without relationship in this mind. Here you are potentially one Mind of God, or the Void, or the basic energy of the

21

universe, the quantum. You can extract or add to the whole.

The unique human field does not merely react or interact; it transacts because it dynamically makes choices. Physicist, Bohn, believes the reason subatomic particles are able to remain in contact with one another regardless of the distance separating them is not because they are sending some sort of mysterious signal back and forth, but because their separateness is an illusion. He argues that at some deeper level of reality such particles are not individual entities, but are actually extensions of the same fundamental something, the Quantum.

As you look at wellness or illness, you can no longer look at it as separate from the dynamics or interactions with consciousness as an entire person. You must see, then look again, and see it in its totality.

Thought gives order to the world of matter. Mind gives meaning to the world of matter. Mind as the observer has dominion over matter. Mind gives the meaning, like looking at a picture of a child on a swing. The brain sees the picture of the child on a swing. Yet, mind gives the meaning of the child's attitude, context, conditions, etc.

If consciousness as thought is the beginning of all being-ness or things, the potential of all dreams, how do we apply this concept to our manifestations and desires? Let's look at what science has to say about thoughts, beliefs and actions.

Chapter 4

If all of the World's a Stage, What's your script?

As a man thinketh, so he is...
Napoleon Hill

How much of what you perceive is illusion and how much is based on fact? **You may be surprised at the answer.** The way the brain processes information is very different from what most people understand.

Beliefs, attitudes, and emotion are the stuff of the mental realm. Thoughts are the ever-present self-talk constantly going through your head—the dialogue with yourself. Some self-talk uplifts, reinforces your strengths and motivates you in becoming successful. We call this positive self-talk. Through self-talk, the conscious mind can influence the subconscious part, which in turn influences behavior subconsciously.

Negative self-talk is the judgmental stuff. It tells you all the reasons why you can't have something you want, it can't be done, it isn't worth it, isn't available to you, or why you're "doomed". Self-talk is like a set of filters, layer upon layer, defining your reality. What you believe to be true; tends to be true, **for you**. What you believe not to be true; tends not to be true, **for you**. If you believe you can or can't—you are right!

The responsibility of these guardians is to evaluate all incoming information trying to get to your brain. These guardians will either allow or deny access to the "Thought Center" (Thalamus) in the brain. Its prime directive is to protect you from making changes too easily that might adversely affect you or your belief. It's like getting into a private club only after your pals carefully evaluated you.

Just imagine this group of pals—very devoted to your brain as a collection of computer programmers. They have their workstations in front of a large bio-computer (your brain) and are on call 24 hours a day, every day of the year, every year of your life, 24/7—never taking vacations or resting. They are your most precious assets, completely devoted to your survival by maintaining what has worked or believed to have work in the past.

Being good pals, they are not purposefully trying to sabotage your efforts. They believe that any new or unfamiliar program is not in your best interest, since it is contrary to many previous instructions received from you in your life. Pals can be seen as the shadows. The shadows cloud the object or situation, so we do not see them as clearly as we could.

These pals are usually formulated in adversity and perpetuated by unwillingness to see or change. Like good guardians, if they have been delegated the task of watching out for falling rocks, left turns, they remain continually attentive to the believed possibility, which keeps it ever in view (attached to the negativity). Learn to look at life as something to be created out of your personal programming and purpose, rather than a maze—of knowledge, beliefs, goals, challenges to be run through like a rat. (See Part II, Releasing Negative Beliefs for a few exercises)

The main concept to remember is that what you believe, you attract into our lives. You can live the life by creating with your thoughts. You can choose to live a life that is a dream or a nightmare. If you believe you are healthy, then it is what you will manifest in our lives. It's all perspective and what you choose to focus on. Choose personal freedom—freedom from societal pressure, guilt, and wrong thinking.

In her book *Heal Your Body*, Louise L. Hay, Science of Mind Minister, Counselor and Teacher, states that **mental thought patterns causing the most disease in the body are criticism, anger, resentment, and guilt.** Ms. Hay gives a quick list of probable mental patterns behind the disease in a body. Indulged in long enough, criticism will often lead to diseases such as arthritis; usually associated with a feeling of being unloved, criticized, and holding resentment. Arthritic fingers, a desire to punish, blame with a feeling of being victimized. Anger manifests in boiling, burning, and infecting the body with skin eruption and boils. Bronchitis is related to inflamed family environment with arguments and yelling and sometimes, silence.

Long held resentment eats and ultimately can lead to tumors and cancer—deep hurts; deep secrets or grief eats away at the self and carries hatreds with a feeling of "what's the use". Guilt seeks punishment, leading to pain or lack.

Alice Steadman, author of *Who's the Matter With Me*, studied in depth the correlation between attitudes and diseases. Her autographed copy sums it up well; an oyster takes an irritation and makes of it a pearl. How many pearls could we make in a week?

It is generally agreed among psychologists today, that your future is largely determined by your present. If you want to change, you must be prepared to think and do something completely different than what was thought or done before—or it's rather foolish to believe you can make any substantial changes in your life.

Either stop reading right now and keep your reality as status quo, or read on to learn how to transform your life. IF you have to argue for your reality, you deserve it.

What's the "trick" that unlocks this door? It is to be willing to make mistakes and learn. Consider your current "pals"—those that brought you to this point in your life, as "myths" or even "misunderstandings." The emotional realm, remember, is your feelings about people, places, events, things, and time.

It's a chemical reaction to your thoughts, beliefs, and expectations about situations that occur in the physical world reality. Energy is action in motion; triggered by thoughts and beliefs.

Picture in your mind, your thoughts as rail cars on a track. A thought of the color blue, may lead to thoughts of baby blue, deepening hues, talcum powder, blue skies, blue dress, blue Monday, or jazz. These are the individual cars that link together to make the thought train of Blue. The connected rail cars do not necessarily have to think of the destination. They only have to follow the track. For instance, if traveling from New Orleans to Seattle, each individual car does not consciously focus on Seattle, Seattle, Seattle. The entire train cruises at the proper speed, halting at all scheduled stops until it reaches its destination, Seattle.

However, most cars in the train of thought may not be very clear. Once the decision is made to go to Seattle, if one rail car is unsure and doubts it has the capacity, time, know-how, and hardware to reach Seattle, it will derail. ("Get off track"!) The doubting car just met a competing thought or pal. Many, operate trains much like this.

Each time you change your mind about our destination or goals you DOUBT; energy gets interrupted. The process has to start all over again, establishing a new track or re-establishing the old one.

In quantum physics the observer, through observation, can create the subjective experience of hopelessness. The observer fuses with, and experientially becomes, this hopelessness and thinks that is who they are. Now, this relates to any judgment, thought, or observation. This is a miss-taken (mistaken) identity. When you become identified with these created aspects, you conclude this is who you are—rather than this is what I constructed to perceive myself. Another way to say it is this is a self-lens that you created, and it will define you and your world, as long as you continue to observe it.

Remember Grandma? How she would listen to you with unconditional acceptance? How she would sit patiently and let you cry, all the while giving you the message that she still loved you, accepted you no matter what—All that wisdom and no Ph.D. or B.S...!

Listening to others, you can listen to yourself with more compassion. How? Consider your emotions as young children who need to be lovingly heard and understood evenly, needing nurture, comfort, and wise guidance. With this understanding, you can now begin to uncover whatever beliefs, thoughts, rules or standards you hold in your mind that are the actual causes of your emotional upset. Remember the shadows do not allow you to see clearly. By re-educating the hurts or wounds, disappointments and misunderstandings of the past, you can reduce their activity to emotional upset and free energy to create a new track to a healthier life.   Change the lens with which you choose to see.

Fear of the unknown is the most limiting fear of all!

I once read a story about African fishermen who, instead of using lines and hooks to catch fish, used the hot African sun filtered through wooden slats to create shadows in the water.   The fish see the shadows and flee. The fishermen repeatedly move the slats, pushing the fish into shallow water so they can easily catch them.   To the fish, these shadows, which are simply an absence of light, are as real as physical walls.

Both real and imagined barriers also prevent most from obtaining desired goals.   Fear of the unfamiliar is the real inhibitor.   Fear and ignorance frequency go hand -in-hand. Even if obstacles are real, what is imaginary is usually their severity.   But once understood, most of these problems can be easily be overcome. By learning to intervene positively and strategically in your physical, mental, and emotional levels, you can free yourself from barriers that keep you from opening yourself to a greater life.   All dreams or goals involve risk, and if you are willing, you can minimize risk to an acceptable point—that is, the point at which risk is acceptable to you.

Deborah Baker-Receniello, PhD, CLSC

Whatever you identify with, you are subject to its effects. What goes around comes around! As the observer, begin to appreciate that you are not your thoughts, feelings, and emotions, just a witnessing presence, a greater clarity emerges.

Each time you are tempted to react in the same old way, ask if you want to be a prisoner of the past or a pioneer of the future. The past is closed and limited; the future is open and free.

Take a few moments before you get out of bed in the morning and just listen to your thoughts. Be the observer of what you are setting up for the day. Change any negative thought into a positive one. Instead of avoiding Sally, next time I see her, I'll smile and say hi. What will Sally's reaction be? Remember, no one actually sees a person as if it were the first time. There are always memories and reactions associated with you. You are prejudged before you enter a room. When you are the observer you can change the way you see others and then change the way you are seen. Many business encounters can benefit from this one.

It's like riding a merry-go-round and waiting to get off -- yet have to wait for the music to end.

What you think about all the time is attracted into your life, whether consumed by **Dislike, Passion, or a Concept.**

It is you that determines your fate and nothing and no one else. Take personal responsibility for your actions and the results in your life. Remember mistakes are only learning situations not a fixed lifestyle. Miss-takes, like a movie scene can be done over and over until it is right. In Zen, to sin is to miss the mark. Missing the mark gives you information to get closer next time.

Whatever you believe with absolute conviction and confidently expect to happen becomes a self-fulfilling prophecy and will become your reality.

The more certainty you add to the energy you send out, the bigger the chance that it will take form in the physical world.

Let's see how the brain works with belief and what you feel, and how to make your dreams come true.

Chapter 5

Brain, Emotion, and Memory

*People have traveled to wonder at the
heights of mountains, huge waves in the sea,
long courses of rivers, vast compass of the
ocean, the circular motion of the stars; and
yet, they pass by themselves without
wondering...*
St. Augustine, 399 A.D.

As you become aware of the invisibility of
creation, you can become a scientist to
understand how to make yourself more aware of
your creative abilities. It's now time to pay
real attention to the world; it's alive. In
other words, science says, you use knowledge
and experience to build a larger, more
expanded model of thought for greater
experiences in life. You question what if?
What are the possibilities? How can I do that
better or differently? How do I make miracles
happen? What makes the extraordinary,
ordinary? This is an internal reality that
science explains through the process of brain
function.

Some think of information as power. Information is only powerful, when it is used or acted upon. If you have teenagers you may hear yourself saying, you have to act on what you know, not just know it. If you know how to make a space ship, it doesn't make you powerful. It could. It is the orchestration of events, circumstances, need, resources, and many other factors necessary to bring the space ship or any project into fruition.

Your marvelous brain can only draw on its stored knowledge—knowledge of preprogrammed intellect, environment, and experiences. This information is interpreted as a set of impulses (frequency) in the brain and can become hard-wired through setting up dendrite connections.

The brain receives information through our senses (sight, sound, touch, smell, taste, and perceived sixth sense) in the form of light impulses (as electrical/chemical impulses through the organs to receptors in the brain). It translates the information and transmits it throughout the body, registering involuntary body reactions.

In the brain, the lower cerebellum houses the subconscious mind where all information is known. Remember, your subconscious received a number of messages from you and it creates reality based on these messages and it doesn't know linear time. The reptilian brain (our beliefs) acts like a clamp and shuts off any new information (light impulses as frequency) that is not stored in the knowledge-bank. When creating it is important to have your thoughts and feelings in agreement with what you visualize, otherwise you'll never create the things that you visualize no matter how you try.

The brain sends and receives information. Like a computer, the cell acts as the hardware with a simple software program inside and around it that tells it what to do. If the system received too much energy, it may burn out the program, causing the cells to run-a-muck. In medicine, that's called disease. What would happen if we could re-install the software or information wave packet back into the system? It would appear that the cells seem to respond and feel happy to get back to work. How does the information get to where it needs to go?

An architect knows all the angles, geometry, design, layout, and is a master builder' taking the vision and translating it into a design (blueprint). Then the contractors proceed to build the home.

The front part of the brain is where pictures (Current, as electromagnetic energy) are stored knowledge in the brain.

Our brain uses a process for generating and transforming energy into reality. You can think of a vision as a mental matrix, blueprint, or model. Then take this holographic matrix or blueprint and transform it with the aid of electrical stimuli (neurons firing in the brain). You need to charge or animate its form with energy (emotion) with chemical-constructs (hormones) and memory from the hypothalamus. The more expanded the emotion or character of the vision, the more energy will be required to bring it into the physical world. Using first the vision or intention, then use concentrated focus to expand or charge with energy. This brings forth more intense desire. With this desire then comes the commitment, which transforms the emotion (energy) into physical force and action.

The realm of ideas is the inner world of thought, imagination, intention and feeling. Things are the physical environment in which we live, our actions, objects and events.

Commitment takes us across the bridge to action, planning, execution and feedback. Commitment is the will to go for what you want and the willingness to let go of things that keep you from getting it. Then the action occurs; those steps we plan and initiate. Then we have the experience. After the experience, we then can build a better model. Take what is known about your experience and using that to make it better. Each time, we create a better model or an evolution of our experiences and models of thought.

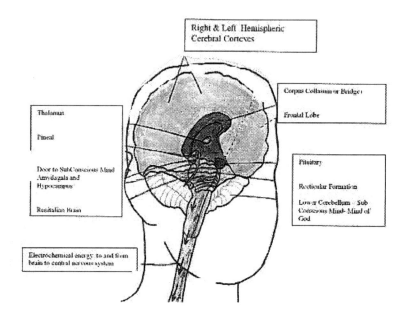

Not drawn to scale

The brain has the capability to receive all seven levels of the electromagnetic spectrum. Within this electromagnetic spectrum are streams of consciousness (information), energy waves, and the atmosphere where the intelligence and energy live. There are seven glands in the brain that correspond with these seven levels of the electromagnetic spectrum. Science now tells us that we are using less than ten percent (10%) of our brain capacity. It doesn't take much brainpower just to keep the body alive. The law of evolution says, you need to use something or you lose it.

Remember body-mind.

These streams enter the brain at the pineal gland, which is like an antenna on a radio. Once there, the pineal signals the thalamus. The thalamus is like a tuner on the radio. It decides which stream of consciousness or intelligence it will allow to go further in the brain, **based on the mind of the person owning the brain, the conscious awareness.** That mind is made up of the beliefs, education, culture, environment, emotion of that owner. If the intelligence is rejected by the thalamus, it stops there. If the streams of consciousness or intelligence is allowed to go beyond the thalamus, it then goes to the pituitary. Then, the pituitary takes the flash of electromagnetic impulse and translates to chemicals to flood the brain and the body.

When you become more consciously aware, the greatest creative forces become more available to you. When you become the observer, you can decide to become more watchful of your thoughts and actions and especially of your dreams. Be deliberate instead of walking about doing things on automatic. You make choices, but if you are not aware of the programs running you, you may not make the choices to match your dreams, when manifesting.

Perhaps in the past, you had indecision or fear about your dream or desire. That will not allow the creative into your sphere of manifestation. That creates more fear and indecision by being the background noise in all that you do. Remember, the creative quantum gives what you think. Make sure your conscious and unconscious thoughts are in agreement, along with your feelings for the complete manifestation of the dream.

In actuality, within the cerebral cortex reside the estimated 100 billion neurons linked by 1 million billion connections. If we would count these connections at the rate of one connection per second, it would take **32 million years** to complete. Even a section of the brain no bigger than a match head contains about a billion connections. Consider that the number of positively charged particles in the whole known universe is only ten followed by 80 zeros. These neurons communicate in combination of electricity and chemistry (neurotransmitters).

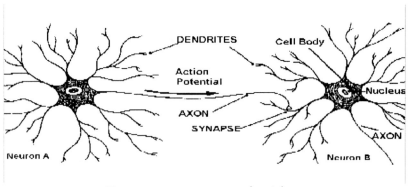

Two neurons communicating

That number is more than the atoms in the universe. Now look at the number of atoms that can fit on the head of a pin - 10 trillion. How many atoms could fit in the palm of your hand? On the chair you are seated upon? The Room? The building? City? State? Country? Planet? Universe? The potential of the brain is greater than all the atoms in the universe.

The brain has the ability of plasticity. The older you get, the nerve cells get rigid and still, that's referred to as "hard wiring" in the brain. If you travel down the road of the same neuron firing with your thought patterns and it is like creating highways and superhighways or a needle stuck in the scratch of an old 33rpm record. Children have more plasticity. If you were to cut a slice of the brain in an adult, the dendrites severed would wiggle like an electric cord that is plugged in the wall and severed at the other end, no place to go and then run out of energy and lay still. In a child, those severed dendrites would wiggle, jump and reconnect.

Often these occur at places called dendrite spines, which are tiny protuberances on dendrites at which contact with synaptic knobs can be made. Here, 'contact' means not just touching, but leaving a narrow gap (synaptic cleft) of just the right distance – about one forty-thousandth of a millimeter. Now under certain conditions, these dendrite spines can shrink away and break contact, or they can grow to make new contact. (Changing the thought or belief, remember the rail cars)

This plasticity refers to how circuits in the brain change—organize and reorganize—in response to experience, sensory stimulation or thought. This is where change takes place.

Neurologically you can make connections to manifest something from no-where! You can make something that is uncommon in your experience or unknown, any everyday experience. When you hook up neurologically, the unrealistic, unlimited, miraculous can become very normal and everyday experience. The discipline is to have knowledge, continue to do it until it clicks, then it happens without thinking—and becomes common thought or accepted reality. It becomes automatic.

Sounds easy, but it isn't! You associate yourself with people, places, things, times and events for survival of the physical body through perceptions by our senses. This becomes the neural original or hard wiring in our brains, as you age. The brain plugs you into this reality, the experience of a third dimensional density.

In the corpus collosum, 300 Million nerve impulses are capable of receiving 400 billion bits of information a second. The eye is capable of seeing 1 trillion bits, awesome. If you had a painting on a wall, say 100 feet long, 20 feet tall, all the dots contained in the picture that makes up the picture would be about 1 trillion bits of information. Say the picture was of Mount Rainier, forest, clouds, sky, children playing, streams, deer, birds, hikers, picnic area, skiers, squirrels, snow, etc. The eye is capable of seeing 1 trillion dots of the painting and the corpus collosum is capable of 400 dots, your awareness is only 2000 dots. Mind lives in a sea of 400 billion bits of information and 1 trillion bits and you are only responding to 2,000 per second.

Consciousness can be physical minded when awareness is set on the body; your back hurts, hat is too tight, hungry, bored, tired, happy, sad, reaction to other physical minded consciousnesses, especially beautiful people.

It's called personality. Science tells us that what you experience consciously shapes your habits and behaviors—how? Knowledge and experience (more information) and how we feel (emotion/energy) connect the neurons to other neurons. Each neuron roughly has 50,000 connections, remember the tree. This is what forms your limitations of social, ethics, nutrition, tradition, behaviors, religion and habits.

The more connections you have, the more ability you have to process data. Einstein had 150,000 connections to each neuron—remember 50,000 normally found. Einstein's brain looked more like trees of linguini and had much more than the normal noodle tree. When he was 11 years, he asked the question, if I were riding my bicycle at the speed of light, if I turned on the light, would I see it? Einstein was a visionary, he had to study science and mathematics to understand his visions. Does that sound familiar?

Contained in the subconscious mind is the intelligence of the smallest (micro-organism) to the greatest (macro-organism), from earth throughout the universes—every past, present and future. If you took a slice of one neuron from this area of the brain, it would have 10 million connections, what would that tree look like?

We learn, memorize, and gather data from all experiences. Three basic laws of mind are ASSOCIATION, REPETITION, and ATTRACTION.

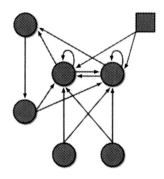

Association: The more you connect thoughts, people, events, etc. the bigger the amount of energy is capable of causing changes. Conscious brain works to identify past experiences (what is known) to build a bigger model of thought. It takes its present knowledge and associates to new information to create a better model. If I were to say apple, most would respond red. The apple is associated with red color. If I said red, some would respond apple and others wine. Remember being a baby. You were hungry, you cried and you got fed. You associated crying with food. Association is the groundwork to accept (FILL IN THE BLANK_____)

Whatever it is, as being ordinary and normal.

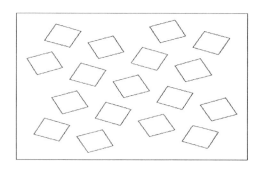

Repetition: Do something over and over and it becomes common or automatic. The more often you think, feel or ponder the same thing the more belief and certainty is raised in your mind.

Think back when you learned any skill—Riding a bicycle or learning to drive for the first time. I remember my first lesson with my mom. She had an 1967 white, Corvair, Chevrolet, blue interior, radio, stick shift, ah...

1. You have some knowledge or information.

   Get behind the wheel. Fasten seat belt. Check mirrors. You are feeling excited. Foot on break and clutch. Turn on blinkers to signal a move into the street. Look! Put into correct drive gear. Slowly remove foot from clutch and slowly give it gas. Hands on wheel, no don't look at me, look at the road. What happens? Watch out for the neighbor's garbage cans. Now, smooth sailing. Oops! I didn't know a mailbox could do that. Drive home. Pull back into the driveway. Peel your gripped fingers from the steering wheel one at a time, not realizing they were fused.

2. Next you review all this experience - going over in your mind about twenty times a minute, correcting, changing or modifying your actions.

3. You've reviewed, changed and perhaps slept on it. Now you get inside the car and start over. Soon, you are not thinking. This non-thinking state is when the subconscious has taken over. The subconscious does not

43

think, yet it acts and has the ability to take over body function without using the left and right hemispheres of the frontal lobe in the brain. How many times, have you driven for a few miles and suddenly realize you weren't there? Where were you and who was driving?

4. It clicks! This non-thinking state is what makes the unfamiliar, common, natural, and easy. In contrast to emotions at the physical body level, in an altered state, there is evidence of an open emotional system that is in touch with deep needs and subtle happenings in the universe. This is a no-time/no-space realm. You discover a free emotional energy, super-consciousness— the home of the peak experiences, ah ha; that we never forget.

ATTRACTION:

The "Law of Attraction" in simplest terms means you get what you think about, what you focus on and what you talk about. Is your balance of thought and communication more on the side of what you want or what you don't want in your life? You only get what you are equal to, until you expand what you are, through experience or education. Like attracts like.

Most people can clearly articulate in great detail, vividness and emotion all the things that are not going right in their lives. They are completely clear about who caused it and why they are so miserable and they are constantly telling anyone who will listen. Do you know someone like this...perhaps you? Is it any wonder why they would continue to attract the same problems and situations over and over again: Same financial situations, relationships, and habits.

Have you ever known anyone who was completely focused on what they desired and seemed to effortlessly attract people and situations into their life as if by magic? The Law of Attraction works to bring you more of what you want or what you don't want simply by your attention to it.

You attract what they are, not what they desire, remember atmosphere. You attract what they love and what they fear. That which you sustain and judge, you are condemned. What you resist persists. What you truly believe is what becomes real in their lives.

Learn to develop the ability of imagination—take knowledge and blend together the building blocks of thoughtful creativity. Then be consumed by that thought. By that consumption, you increase our level of acceptability. That thought will disturb the electromagnetic field and dissolve the old dendrite connections and become liquid, only to create new connections. The imagination will set up the state of mind and body coagulates, not as it was, but as you intend.

IMPORTANT: Visualization, imagination and meditation act to mobilize the molecules of emotion for specific tasks such as the shrinking of a tumor, manifestation of a desire, the reduction of stress, or linking to the Mind of God, Void, or quantum.

Visualization is like remembering an apple. What's the color? Is it ripe or sour? Does it have a bruise or can you see the grain? Imagination is taking what is already know about the apple and changing it to something else. A blue apple, with white stripes. Meditation is focusing on a concept or idea and letting it present to you its qualities, beyond what is known.

Roger Penrose in his book, *The Emperor's New Mind*, states; it is actually not legitimate to regard the brain as simply a fixed collection of wired-up neurons. The interconnections between neurons are not in fact fixed, but are changing all the time. Reference is to the synaptic junctions where the communication between different neurons actually takes place. This is the world of quantum physics.

The brain analyses its environment to either move you toward what is comfortable (feels good) and move away from what makes you uncomfortable (feels bad or threatened) based on your past.

Pain <————   ————> Pleasure

This defines our limitations or our realm of acceptability. If we are to make known the unknown (the desired manifestation) and the unknown represents a threat and you're uncomfortable, you have just hit a wall of limitation. The limitation is the greatest reality you can be! It is believed to be the only reality. The good news is you can change it.

Every attitude of living responds to a certain vibratory influence or frequency. You live on those very planes by the very attitude you take toward those conditions. Therefore, you progress only as our thoughts progress. The moment you doubt, you put up a wall. That wall cannot be penetrated until it is dissolved in your thoughts. Here you declare your truth (the new design or manifestation) completely, friendly and determined.

When you wake-up to realize (make real) that you are all powerful beings intermingling with each other's lives in a vast sea of probability and possibility; what could the next moment reveal? Could enlightenment be "contagious"? Could perfect health, wealth, love, or genius?

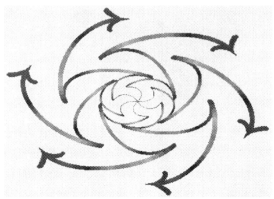

You are the center, the observer, collapsing the
wave function by your images, emotion,
and certitude = your reality!

How is reality created in the brain?

Remember driving down the road or being immersed in a task for 45 minutes. You were completely unaware of the environment and somewhere else? Where were you? For those moments, *the picture in your mind is more real than the outside world reality.* You lose track of time. You slipped into that subconscious mind, analogically; you were in your past, immersed in people, places, things, time and events. When analogical, you are no longer assessing the immediate environment or time.

The brain doesn't know time. The brain operates outside the box of personality. There is a moment when you focus on something long enough that the image freezes and is pushed to the frontal lobe of the brain. The subconscious mind has hook ups to the frontal lobe and endorses the image into reality.

Quantum physics, Planck's theory, says time flows in all directions and like the movie we see; is not really moving but appears to. Each time packet flashes on and off. It's as though thought is frozen bits of the quantum time. It happens very quickly, thus the illusion of moving forward. The past, present and future exist simultaneously at the quantum level. (See Appendix 4)

I recently watched a video entitled: *The Powers of Ten.* Using visual images along with narration illustrating the relative size of things in the physical universe. First, takes the viewer from a man at a picnic and projects one square inch to the 10th power every 10 seconds—earth to the outer galaxies, showing the increase of time and distance in increments of ten. Then returning to earth proceeds inside the man scale into the micro world of cells, DNA molecules, and the nucleus of a carbon atom, the quantum. The whole video is only 20 minutes. Yet, we managed to move faster than the speed of light from earth to the far reaches of the galaxy and back to the quantum level to the nucleus of a carbon atom. If we tried to do that physically, we do not have the apparatus of travel or the time to get from A to B and back again for anyone to recognize us. The power of the mind is extraordinary. This video is an eye opening experience.

Remember Einstein's Relativity; the distinction between past, present and future is only an illusion, however persistent. When you sit with a nice girl for two hours, you think it's only a minute. But when you sit on

49

a hot stove for a moment, you think it's two hours. That's relativity.

You are bombarded everywhere in our society to programming; music, beats, words, advertising, etc. The brain translates these as "right NOW!" No yesterday or no tomorrow. Messages are translated in the brain as now. I feel pain, I feel depressed, I'm happy, or I need to buy this product, now. Now, I smell popcorn and I need it. Now I see cookies, I want it now. Get It. No wonder we are exhausted. No wonder our bodies are in chaos.

The brain responds to electrical charges associated with its memory and does not know the difference from a situation happening in the present on a physical level, a memory, a daydream, or "active imagination".

To illustrate this point:

Take a moment after reading this paragraph, close your eyes so that the reality perceived by the five senses is no longer an influence. Remove the current visual reality by closing your eyes. Just the ability to do that is very powerful. You can, literally, make your world disappear—it's your world, remember.

Imagine you are standing in your kitchen. Walk over to the refrigerator. Inside you see a nice, plump juicy lemon. Take it out of the refrigerator. Notice the bumpy, yellow skin (perhaps it is a little waxy and cool to the touch). Walk to the cabinet and get a cutting board. Place the lemon on the cutting board. Grab a sharp knife, cut the lemon in half. See and feel the juice squirts out in every direction, on the cutting board, the cabinet, and all over your hands. Pick up the lemon and smell it. You know it must be tart. Now, squeeze a few drops on your tongue. Taste it.

Now, if you did all those things, you should be salivating or at the very least, puckering-up. This is a bio-physical reaction to a mental thought—active imagination—memory firing neurons as light impulse, translated into an electro- chemical reaction in your own body. You have created an electro-chemical reaction in your own body that did not occur by biting an actual lemon! If you told someone that you are salivating as a result of tasting an imaginary lemon, they would want to know where is the lemon. However, in order for this imagined biological response to occur, you must have a memory of what a lemon looks like, how it tastes, and smells, and what it feels like.

A memory, when combined with active imagination, triggers a physiological reaction in your body. It is, therefore, natural to believe that you can change a situation—there are choices. Active imagination and strong, focused will (attention) is a way to create an image in order to have the physical body respond and accept a new memory. Once a physical response is created, the physical body will now have a newly created memory from which to draw. Building new and greater models of thought equals a new reality. You are in control. You are not your habit and you are running this show. Modify your situation with association and repetition to build the model that is acceptable to equal a greater experience.

Being analogical thought is equal to forgetting about yourself and being fully there—whatever you are thinking or doing; To be in a now moment.

Sounds simple! Yes. Easy? No. Being addicted to your identity according to people, places, things, times and events, keeps your identity in tack. If you live this way, you are separate from the whole of life. Let's take a closer look at the biology of our emotions.

Chapter 6

Biology of Emotion & Creating Health

The fountains mingle with the river
And the rivers with the ocean
The winds of heaven mix forever
With a sweet emotion; Nothing in the
World is single, all thing by a law divine
In one another's being mingle, Why not I?
...P B Shelley Love's Philosophy

Dr Hans Selye developed the Theory of Relaxation (homeostasis in the body and what happens within the body when it is not within that normality). He called it the "Fight or Flight Syndrome." For example, if you were out in the wilderness and confronted by a grizzly bear, you would feel an enormous rush of adrenaline spurring the sensation to fight (to conquer the beast) or flight (run for your life).

Today your beasts are more likely to be deadlines, projects, unreasonable loss, stormy relationships, plummeting stock market, feeling out of control, the challenges of earning a living, buying a home, vehicle, food, security, and children. Today the terms "anger" and "depression" are used more often than "fight" or "flight." Stress and the fight-or-flight syndrome emerge when one's needs are not being met, which relates to expectations and judgments. These attitudes form the basis of our body's ability to respond to stressful situations.

Addition to stress or to emotions puts us, in a moment, ready to stay and fight or run. In this state we use adrenaline to stay and fight or run. Adrenaline is very potent. It gives fuel to muscles for them to take action. Now, socially, fighting is not acceptable and running doesn't solve anything. Here's the dilemma. As humans, we then begin to analyze the solution (rationalize = to make real). Adrenaline moves into the muscles, the body stiffens and the muscles never get used. We then complain of stiffness and inability to move freely. The problem occurs when we associate the hit of adrenaline as a feeling of being alive and active with the environment. We translate this hit as; stress feels good, thereby, creating the addition to feed off the adrenaline.

Corticoids and Steroids take the pain away. They ease the muscles and we feel relaxed... ah...

When stress builds or this process is repeated, eventually the physical body is compromised.

1. Changes in the size of our brain in the area of emotional perception.
2. Fear and Stress reduces the blood flow to our forebrain, where intelligence is active. When feeling joy and love, the forebrain is increased so you have heightened ability to think, create and process information.
3. The immune system is compromised by cortisol and can potentially make cancer worse.
4. Digestion is compromised—disrupts blood supply to organs.
5. Cardiac system changes.
6. Breakdown occurs in the tissues, joints and bones.

The body begins to live in lack, starvation and breakdown. The job is too much to handle. The relationship is not working. How can I pay the bills—The drama of life goes on and on and on, just to get the HIT of adrenaline! If you don't have enough drama in our own life, you can watch television, perhaps tune in to THE DRAMA station. Look at these symptoms, allergies, heart problems, chronic fatigue, osteoporosis, -- Do these sound familiar—these are the ailments of our society?

Scenario: You are feeling a little stressed, tired, out of sorts, you make an appointment with your doctor. Once there, you are told that a vacation might be good. Just take some time off, forget about everything and relax for a few days or weeks. Yes! Now you have permission. You tell your boss and co-workers that you are off for a week. Don't take any Calls! You go home, make some arrangements and pack. You wake up the next morning and the sun is shinning. It's off to the beach. You get inside your car, put the top down and take off. While driving along the coast you have your favorite music playing, wind in your hair, and you enjoy the scenery. Soon, you begin to feel uneasy. *You haven't had an adrenaline hit for hours.*

You begin to think of last week's meeting. You remember how Susie cut you off and Ben took the opportunity to mention your idea that you discussed with him. You remember the reorganization of management or the budgets cuts you have to enact. Wow! Now, enter the *stress, anger and feeling passed over or betrayed or even resentment.*

You are creating chemistry in the mind. Remember the lemon. You are not physically at work. No stress driving through nature's beautiful scenery. You chose to go into the file cabinet of the brain, the hippocampus, and pulled out the stress file. Now you are having the smorgasbord of chemistry. There is no time or space in this memory or reality, except what you make it. It is not happening in a now time, except in your brain. HOWEVER, now the brain gives you a now chemistry feast in a now body. Now you are exhausted as you drive into the cabin driveway.

Tired? Did you do anything? Yes, but it wasn't real! It was a memory, which dumped a now-chemical-feast in the body.

The next time this happens or you find you are with someone else doing this, why not stop. Just stop and begin to associate with the environment, music, whatever, and not the memory (file cabinet in the brain). The body drums it up for the addictive hit of adrenaline because it craves it.

When you need a vacation, it could be fifteen minutes or a week. How about fasting from our emotions. Seeing and being seen has its own chemistry, as well. Every person, place, thing, time and event has been stored in memory, molecules of emotion each with its own chemistry signature. Emotions are hard wired in the gray matter of the brain. It is in the form of a downloadable chip—the hippocampus and it is repeated as a known-over and over again, because it feels good. If you continue to review the wrong things, it is hardwired chemically and it shapes your future behaviors.

Emotions color our reality and result in complex electrochemical interactions within and between nerve cells. Feelings of worthlessness and self-hatred that accompany depression although they seem to be based on reality are no more than distortions in brain electro-chemistry or miss-taken identities.

It's very natural and easy for the brain to play out what is hard wired and accustomed to doing, remember those PALS. The brain is always at work because that is its job. It must keep the body going and feeding it what it needs, without judgment. Unless we find the switch and use other parts of our brain, we can get stuck in the same old, same old. It takes great courage to look a negative emotion in the eye and see it for what it is, a need for a fix.

How then do you balance yourself? The body uses chemicals in the form of corticoids released to kill pain or reduce the stress. Remember every emotion has a chemical signature. The hypothalamus signals to the pituitary gland, which signals to other glands, which signals the release of chemicals into the bloodstream to each individual cell.

The cell:

Each cell has receptor sites. These have been referred to a lock and key system. There is a receptor site for every emotion. The chemicals in the blood will meet the cell receptor. An electrical message is sent to the DNA in the nucleus of the cell and the DNA begins to unwind to look for the chemical signature that matches the electrical message. If it is anger, it looks for an anger chemical.

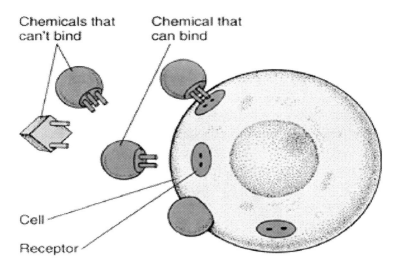

Cell with receptor sites

The body is a protein-producing machine. What you eat changes into amino acids that line up and make proteins. The proteins line up like pearls on a string to form whatever is needed in the nucleus of the cell.

The DNA unravels into a river of muscle proteins to produce muscle cells. DNA unravels into a river of skin protein to make skin cells, etc. Imagine a flash, a picture in the brain; then the flash matches the emotion. Say, it is anger. Then the DNA unravels into a sea of proteins, look for new bone proteins. It finds bone proteins and anger proteins. Now, the new chain begins...

X Bone protein + Y anger protein + X bone protein + Y anger = XY new bone, however, mutated and weakened by the chemistry of anger Not as the original X bone.

Now you have new bone cells that are not at their best. Science calls this down regulation of cells. These then do the process over and over and each time they become weaker and weaker. The cell wall receptors get wired for more anger and less nutrition causing weakness of the cell replication. This can lead to osteoporosis. Those of you that understand photography know that you can take a print and copy it. With each copy it fades depending on the equipment used to make the copy. It is a form of replicatative fading.

There are 300 Billion nucleotides in DNA and you use about 3%. This 3% determines mostly your appearance, hair color, eye color, etc. You have 97% that is still available to you. This other 97% could be the nucleotides for genius, longevity, invisibility, better modeling in the brain, health, being in two places at once, etc. For further research, see *Molecules of Emotion*, by Candice Pert.

If you live in fear and weakness for thirty years unraveling the DNA in the bone cell—collagen levels weakens, flexibility weakens and strength weakens. When you live in greed for thirty years unraveling the DNA, the result could be diabetes. Living without compassion could lead to weakened heart muscle and functions.

Roger Penrose, renowned mathematician and Dr. Stuart Hameroff, anesthesiologist, believe they have found the biology of mind. It is in the Microtubules. Microtubules (MTs) are the molecular filament or cytoskeleton of the neurons. These dissolve and reform according to consciousness, just like the caterpillar and the butterfly, reducing a tumor, and creating genius.

The microtubules act like railway tracks for the rapid transport of material away from and back to the cell body. In his book *Shadows of the Mind,* Penrose gives a compelling argument to support the theory that quantum coherence, made possible by the microtubulin cytoskeleton of neuronal cells, is the necessary ingredient to transform consciousness into the electro-chemical process exhibited in the brain.

The electromagnetic field (matrix or blueprint) creates molecules and chemicals. They combine to create the cells, which combine to create tissues, then organs, systems of organs and finally the whole organism. Thought creates the collapse of the function (making something out of nothing).

THE GOOD NEWS

If you learn to alter the emotion, you can alter the body.

The cells replicate - they can either better themselves or down regulate the next generation-- alter to have the chemistry to match the picture in brain = altered body.

The nucleus of the cell contains 50% DNA and 50% protein. The nucleus is not in control of the cell, according to Dr. Bruce Lipton Cellular Biologist. Protein is the building blocks of the structure of cell linking amino acids like beads on a string. The length of the amino chain and the sequence of the amino acids determines the function. The environment sends signals to the receptor of the cell which can change the shape of the amino acid chain, which in turn changes the behavior of the cell—all through our perception.

Perception controls our genes. Evolutionary changes adapt to the environment. What's your environment? What are your beliefs of the environment? Perception controls our genes, determines our cell behavior and rewrites our genes according to it's view. Perception is a filter of what is actually happening at any given time. If we perceive our environment as hostile, we move into a mode of protection. This compromises the body in many ways, already discussed. If we perceive our environment as safe and loving we move to growth and immortality.

Knowledge is power and lack of knowledge is no power. Life offers everything and you will only see what the filters allow. How important is this?

Perception = attitudes and beliefs coupled with emotion

Attitude, beliefs and emotion produce peptides in the brain (chemical Messengers/hormones)

These chemical messengers/hormones plug into receptor sites on the cell

Accepted hormones produce action within the nucleus and determines the function of that cell (behavior)

Behavior (expression in DNA) = Health and evolution or protection and disease

ATTITUDE = health, wealth, joy, love, compassion, success and

ATTITUDE = YOU! You see, attitude/perception is everything!

If attitude is everything, we now have tools to effectively change.

Emotion is the basis of learning, reasoning, and helps us to adapt to a complex, rapidly changing environment. Emotion, then, can help us navigate the intimate relationship between our private conscious feelings and our biological survival. Using this tool, what could it mean for your creativity, innovation and free will.

You can understand how you create negative, as well as, positive results. The process is exactly the same. If you have been unaware in the past, you can now become more conscious or aware of your thoughts and feelings. If you want to change, you must feed our brains with new knowledge and then choose to use that new knowledge in a new way. Have a new you! Have a new job! Have a new relationships, house, or travel home! When we begin to learn we can release the past and give energy to something new or an unknown experience. You can begin to dream outrageous thoughts and prepare for the experience. You prepare our physical, body to walk into the new experience. You learn to disassociate with people, places, things, times and events with their negative emotional charge to FOCUS ON ANYTHING, to BE ANYTHING, or DO ANYTHING.

Make your choices count. Practice every time you can and this allows the miraculous to occur.

A memory, when combined with active imagination, triggers a physiological reaction in your body. Remember the lemon, It is, therefore, natural to believe that you can change a situation—there are choices.

Active Imagination and strong, focused will (attention) is another way to create an image in order to have the physical body respond and accept a new memory. Once a physical response is created, the physical body will have a new memory from which to draw.

Suppose you want to change a belief or habit. Let's look at what the program (grid-lock) of your memory of the habit is and how it has attached itself to many things in your life. This process is defined as being the OBSERVER or the SILENT WITNESS, which means becoming more aware. Habit and beliefs are attached to awakening in the morning with a craving or the belief. How about that first cup of coffee? Is it attached to certain foods or eating time? Is it associated with going to a dead end job? I don't want to get up? It's Monday! What else is associated? Negativity has just taken hold and released its chemicals in starting your day.

When you have a "hunger" for any of these emotions, you will go for the habit because it has been associated with all of these.

How does the habit change? To reroute the associations or change the gridlock program of "I am habit or belief to "I am a new habit or belief how must you change? How will the change affect your life? Are you willing to make the necessary changes? Learn to do what you want, however, only, do that thing. Each association has to be addressed. Begin by picturing yourself in the imaginative play of a mental movie of all those situations associated, then edit it to exclude the unwanted behavior; bring up a feeling of joy and satisfaction. See yourself in the situation. When the brain accepts this new scene, you will no longer crave the habit or belief,(See techniques in the back of the book). When looking at habits, additions or beliefs to change, it is important to remember:

Impatience is a habit.
Wrong thinking is a habit.
"I can't" is a habit.
Shoud is a habit.

When we begin to explore habits, we find we have many.

Suppose something has happen in your life that was tragic.

Recalling this event from your memory triggers associated emotions such as pain, regret, guilt or fear. You desire to change it because it prevents you from doing something you want to do.

The reason you may not be abundant is because there is no memory of abundance in your life. If your experience is always to have been in lack, there is no presence of abundance. The brain does not have any information to act on to be abundant. To change that, a new memory has to be created. To create it, use your imagination. Go back to the past and create a new scene in your movie. Now, by doing this, you can live a future moment.

See every option and opportunity possible and deliberately plan for every potential. Live a future event, AND do it in a now moment. The brain only knows a now, present moment. Now, with a memory of a future event acting on your present moment, this gives you a physiological response in the now moment, which becomes a past event in the brain...a memory. As long as one lives in the past, that memory is creating the present moment, because the brain only acts on what information is being imprinted at each moment.

If a patient sees any treatment as violent, then the body will be flooded with negative emotions and the chemicals associated with them. It is well documented that in a climate of negativity, the ability to heal is greatly reduced—depressed people not only lower their immune response, but also even weaken their DNA's ability to repair itself.

MEMORY

How powerful are beliefs? It's magic or a curse. As a psychotherapist working with cancer and cardiac patients, I witnessed that if physicians did not believe that a patient's involvement with hypnosis, creative imagery, subliminal tapes or the belief that the patient's attitude could affect the cancer, the patient usually was affected by the doctor's attitude negatively and regardless of the treatment used (radiation, chemotherapy, surgery)—the treatment was perceived as negative, as well.

For those physicians who agree that the mind plays an important role in patient's health (in varying degrees), then the survival/remission rate increased to 55% in our office. The figures increased further when the patient and the doctor strongly believed the patient had control of his/her body to as much as 100%. Apparently, individuals rely too heavily on opinions of authority (whomever you give your power) to prove them correct.

Could a belief or attitude such as, "Life is like a pain in the butt" produce colon cancer? Could "It's a pain in the neck" produce an injury there? If a "Situation is staggering in the mind", can it cripple the body? Some initial attitudes and mind-sets of clients were:

1. " I always felt unworthy and disappointed. My husband got a girlfriend. I got cancer and he became attentive and stayed home." During chemotherapy, he would bring me

chocolates and read to me and tend to my needs. When he strayed, I had re-occurrences.

2. "My husband committed suicide. I thought I failed him and no longer felt like a woman. I had a mastectomy one year later."

3. "I have a genetic disposition to cancer and lived in fear. Those circumstances got the best of me. Then, cancer, only to find, that I did have reasons to live.

4. "I just could not tolerate anything— circumstances caved in on me. I was a wealthy man with every material thing one could imagine. Anger consumed me as my wealth grew because of other people around me and their reactions to me." This patient had two massive tumors the size of oranges on each side of his lungs, which protruded through his ribcage. He died of respiratory failure because of increased doses of morphine.

5. "With my background of being raped when I was five and being a battered child, it was no wonder I manifested cancer. I went into total panic when diagnosed. I remembered reading about someone who used their mind to heal and looked for a counselor right-a-way."

In one family, (all living in the same house, eating the same food) within a short seven-year period, five out of six developed cancer—the only exception was each developed different kinds: One had colon cancer; one ovarian; another had a mastectomy; yet another skin cancer; and the last an automobile accident with whiplash and cervical cancer of the neck. Each found to be linked to differing mental attitudes. Only one did not develop any form of cancer (much to a cantankerous nature, I suppose).

If, memory affects the immune system, what happens with that seasonal cold or an anniversary of a serious illness or traumatic accident? I had many patients come back near the anniversary with ailments or behavior patterns that resembled those at the time of their initial illness or accident. It was a strong memory of the past event that triggered the similar or exact symptoms. The brain responds to this memory and creates "a now" situation with the same physiological, mental, and emotional states at the time of the illness or injury.

Candace Pert, neuroscientist and chief of brain biochemistry for the National Institute of Mental Health, confirmed with PET scans that the hippocampus, played a crucial role in memory; it's our file cabinet or memory chip. The hippocampus is the area of the brain, which, together with the limbic system, modulates the immune system. Pert suggested that, that neuropeptides are so basic that they exist even in single-celled life. There are 50 or 60 known neuropeptides, which are made directly from the DNA. The neuropeptides link the nervous system, endocrine system and immune system flow of information and adapt accordingly.

Emotions are a key element in self-care. They allow us to enter into a body/mind conversation. By listening to the emotion and directing them through psychosomatic network, we gain healing wisdom that is everybody's biological right.

In his best-selling story, *The Anatomy of an Illness*, Norman Cousins tells of recovery from a crippling and supposedly irreversible disease, of a partnership between physician and patient who team to beat the odds. He decided to stay in the hospital and gather funny movies. He laughed himself to health. Cousins is a senior lecturer at the School of Medicine, at U.C.L.A. and affiliated with the Saturday Review of Literature.

Dr. Deepak Chopra, in *Quantum Healing*, stated patients at the edge of despair, struggling for hope, do replace fear and uncertainty with the memory of health. Chopra was born in New Delhi, India and taught at Tufts University and Boston University Schools of Medicine and became chief of staff at New England Memorial Hospital.

I had the pleasure of training with Carl Simonton, a radiation oncologist and pioneer in the study of mind-body techniques for treating cancer. Simonton, along with Stephanie authored the best-selling book, *Getting Well Again*. I highly recommend this book. There are lots of imagery for dealing with cancer and disease.

The brain is like a bio-computer and who is the programmer? You are! You can be limited by our past experience, education, religion or political beliefs or you can be as unlimited as you venture to become. There is no age to learning, contemplative thought, the mundane or loftiness. It is a choice.

Only 2% of neuronal communication is electrical and across a synapse. The other 98% of neuronal communication is chemical and mediated by small chains of amino acids called peptides and a special class of those peptides called cytokinins.

If then, your mental-emotional state determines your health by determining which of these peptides and cytokinins are produced, Why not let the neuropeptides of joy massage and permeate our being? Perhaps laughter and good thoughts keep you healthy! What if there was a God Particle or a God peptide?

Since the brain does not know time. You can use a memory positively to evoke a change in a now moment. You can use a memory by recalling a time when you were vital, strong, and healthy to change your present situation of health -to your new future healthy body. If you don't have a memory, use visualization or imagination to create a memory. Sounds like a miracle? Is love an emotion?

Chapter 7

What's Love Got To Do With It?

The Drop that wrestles in the Sea—
Forgets her own locality—
As I—towards Thee.
                    ...Emily Dickinson

Webster defines emotion as: 1) disturbance, excitement, 2) affective aspect of consciousness; feeling, a state of feeling, psychic and physical reaction subjectively experienced as a strong feeling and physiologically involving changes that prepare the body for action.

Academia defines emotion as having yielded two approaches: emotion as experience and emotion as physiological process. Today, The human mind is envisioned as an energy field organized by emotion, where emotion is an agitation, a disturbance in the quality of flow of energy (POSITIVE OR NEGATIVE) occurring as a result of field transaction. It is energy in motion triggered by thoughts and beliefs. The universe is made of energy. If you look at what emotion means, "E" means outward. Therefore E-motion means outward motion. The physiological phenomena are secondary responses. You may not understand all about emotions, but we do know that all human experiences are created by, stem from, and are embedded in the energetic part of the energy field we describe as emotions.

Emotion is aroused energy, a power source... external stimuli coupled with you thoughts, beliefs, expectations about situations. It is a chemical reaction to stimuli, which occurs in the physical reality.

Look at a negative emotion, like anger—you would discover if you remove the label of "anger", you would feel just a movement of energy moving through your physical body. What happens is that the energy that would normally move through your body is labeled "anger" and probably "bad". Once you, as the observer, label this energy in any way, you put a boundary around it, you contract because it keeps the experience bounded and creates an air of resistance, as opposed to seeing it as energy, which is the basic substance of this E-motion.

In psychology, you can reframe the experience, such as "anger" or "anxiety" as a motivator or an internal barometer that lets you know, that something needs to get done. Then the feeling is seen differently, a process of de-labeling—taking off the labels and seeing emotions as energy. This provides a sense of how the mind is always changing its mind, so to speak. When you identify with each and every thought, you ride an emotional roller coaster. Learning to observe and witness takes more and more of the tumult out of daily experience. The mind will still generate its geyser of every-changing wants, opinions and demands, but the "you" that observes your mind will develop an equilibrium. Instead of whipping through the day on a roller coaster of every thought and emotion, you will begin to glide on still waters, choosing your destination.

The point in the quantum perspective is not to separate yourself from emotions and feelings via denial or dissociation, but to observe and acknowledge them, experience them fully as you observe and notice their boundaries in your mind's eye. What limits are defined? Have the ability to use this to make a better model of tomorrow.

Emotion at the physical body level can be an altered state, there is evidence of an open emotional system that is in touch with deep needs and subtle happenings in the universe. This is a no-time/no-space realm. You discover a free emotional energy, a super consciousness—the home of the peak experiences that we never forget. This reveals a broad continuum of emotions that explain things we knew about ourselves, particularly the schisms in our awareness.

Emotions connect us with self and are the synthesizing mechanism of the body and the emotions connected with the soul are the organizing medium for the mind. Here we learn our own identity, patterns for handling reality and ideally, we should be able to focus on any aspect without blocking any other aspect of reality.

All emotion should flow in a continuum, one merging into the next. Because emotions, the guardians, determine how our mind-field is organized, you generally hang on to one reality at one time while hanging on to another under different circumstances. Ideally, you can focus consciousness on any portion of the spectrum without losing our identity within the larger system to be able to experience emotion materially, spiritually and intellectually process them simultaneously.

Webster defines **love** as: 1. strong affection for another arising out of kinship or personal ties, 2. Attraction based on sexual desire; affection and tenderness felt by lovers, 3. Affection based on admiration, benevolence or common interests, warm attachment, enthusiasm or devotion, 4. Object of attachment, devotion or admiration, 5. Unselfish, loyal, and benevolent concern for the good of another; 6. A person's adoration of God. 7. An amorous episode or inspired by affection.

What's this thing called love? Ever wonder does love really make the world go around? In Greek, there are several words to describe love:

> Philia
>> Eros
>>> Storge
>>>> Agape'

In English, we have such words as:

Love   **LOVE**
    Love   love   and   *love.*

What is really meant by this word "love"? Is it the love of friendship, and companions. Is it the love of family? Is it of passion, powerful and compelling? Is it like pilgrims along the way of a journey that is sacred or of like mind? Is it sacred, as reverently dedicated or devotion? Is it the love of God? Only you know what you mean when you say, "I love you".

What if love has to do with wholeness, like being in the center of a whole that encompasses everything? What if it means you are one with the void, Mind of God or Quantum? You can certainly feel love when you are centered or at the center. If you promptly fall out of love, there is a judgment or expectation that is not fulfilled. The judgment or expectation takes you out of the love (whole), and fractures the circle. Thus, you are separate or fragmented, which can lead to all kinds of negative feelings.

In psychology, the term 'part' refers to an aspect of our individual personality. In quantum physics the concept of the part-ticle can be seen as a part of the unbroken wholeness of the quantum world. Like a part of a person, a part-ticle is part of the whole. Our personality is a part of our being—ness, not the whole. Once you identify with a fracture or part you become limited and cut-off from the whole, feeling heavy, empty, lost, or separate. Through the rigidity of boundaries and the process of fusion and identification, you lose the lightness we seek.

When you honor yourself, you honor others. When you love yourself, you love others. Honoring means to see the beauty, connection, strengths and weakness in each of us while remaining in the center. To be like a star in the universe, shinning outwardly to all that care to share in that light.

What do quantum physics and love have in common?

In the wildly different realms of atoms and intimate relationships, our thoughts alone can create undeniably real affects. In quantum experiments when you change your mind, you literally change the state of matter itself. Imagine, then, how deeply your thoughts can affect your relationships.

With quantum physics you can begin to look at your relationships from an entirely different perspective. It is what you are thinking that silently guides all of your feelings and behaviors and that by working intelligently with those thoughts, you can create a deeper connection and intimacy with those you love.

At the heart of all relationship issues lie in two basic fears: the fear of losing one's self, and the fear of losing the other. Can you overcome these fears simply by "sharing your feelings" or working on what you say and do? If you want real change to occur, you must learn to see beyond your ego or "small self" – and open your awareness to the vast "field of intelligence" that permeates everyone and everything around you.

In a relationship, true love is the ability to be centered within one's true self (devoid of ego) and seeing the other as equal in the center of their true self (devoid of ego). Ego (judgment) limits by letting one above the other or in control of the other is some way. When you heal a relationship you heal yourself, you forgive, and find yourself. This is the instant that pure love infuses and overpowers all separation and there is a pure flow of being.

Remember the ground of all being—The Void, Mind of God – When you are whole, you have lots more to work with. With manifesting this gives us full power instead of identifying with fractured parts and getting only fractured parts of our manifestation.

What if love is a frequency or state of being and not an emotion? Why it is so easy to fall into or out of love? You can be in love when you oscillate at the same frequency and fall out of love when dissonant. Physics tell us again that opposites attract in the three-dimensional world.

The opposites of things fracture the whole and the opposite of things struggle to become whole. Likes often attracts in the fourth-dimensional world. Being centered.

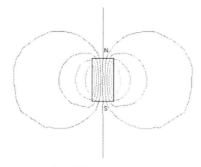

Could love be defined as that which holds all things together? That which you think about all day long is a good indication of what you love, even if it is your enemy.

When you drop the pretense of that which separates you from anything—fear, judgments, prejudices, unknowns, you become larger. It is like taking a few steps back and looking at the whole picture and seeing all the parts; yet knowing it's all reflecting parts of the whole or dimensions of the whole. This is true in relationships and our relationship to our desired outcome or manifestation.

Like the Zen story of each person feeling isolated, when standing in a small circle, each seeing themselves as the only one. Sitting in a tree, you see two and can draw a circle larger to encompass the two.

The world you hold within yourself is your reality. The Kingdom of God is within you. The radiation takes place within you. The entire transmutation process takes place within consciousness; then, all else is made anew.

The human brain received coded information in the form of frequency. It freezes a frequency and creates the coded message. What if love, is the entire electromagnetic spectrum – all the frequencies, at once. Imagine you as a human surrounded by a field of energy floating in a larger field of energy. As the human you can vibrate at the frequency of love or the frequency of that which is termed, separate, fear, guilt, envy, etc.

The reason romantic love makes one feel so safe is not that another person is there to guard you, however, it's that **love** is there to guard you. You are already safe! You are already loved. Fear is only the projection from the past, and as long as there are projections, you will keep generating fearful situations to accommodate them. Fear is a frequency! It dresses in clothes of abandonment, rejection, failure, loss, betrayal, suffering, pity, victim, pain and humiliation.

To give up a life of constant reaction—reacting to effects and outer stimulus with fear, anger, depression and futility, to embody another frequency is a great gift. Harmony is a resonant frequency. Joe is a resonant frequency. Abundance is a resonant frequency. Energy seeks its level just as water seeks its level.

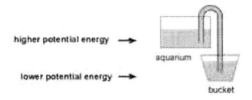

That's the law of displacement. The identity that you are living always goes before you to create the experience of that identity because the energy flowing through you assumes that identity.

One thing to dismiss is that being spiritual on the planet earth is boring, tedious, unfulfilling, sacrificing and blessedly poor. What if the Divine manifests in your life and you become complete with joy, serenity, abundance, and peace, and sovereignty reigning supreme? Remember, nature likes to keep its possibilities open, and therefore follows every possible path. Only when observed is nature forced to choose only one path, so only then is just one path taken.

When you change your thoughts, you begin to radiate a magnetic field. This field can be intensified and broadened. When you practice radiating, we then work with the Law of Attraction of likes. At this level, there are no dualities or opposites. All people, events, situations, condition and circumstances that correspond to our awareness are brought to us through this law. All that you think, all day long, blend into an overall frequency. When you take another view, we step outside of ourselves, as you know it. Get a grander view. In that grander view, there is room for everything, and you can sit in the center as wholeness. "My father's house has many kingdoms"...may take on a new meaning.

Compassion depends on clear-minded understanding. When I am heartbroken, and if I am not frightened, I am able to serve. I often pondered the difference between equanimity and indifference. I have wondered if my response is genuine wisdom or just numbness.

There is a Zen story about an abbot, threatened by a samurai who said, "I could run you through with a sword without blinking an eye." The abbot's response, "I could be run through with a sword without blinking an eye." Do you think this abbot was so clear about the truth that he was unattached to life?

I believe he was not frightened and was able to stay present, in the moment. Fearlessness inspires. It's the attachment to fear and suffering that causes us to suffer. He also understood his true nature was not his physicality, alone. I am sure that the essence of a clear mind is impartial loving, kindness and unwavering compassion. I know I can act unskillfully when I am confused by anything, especially fear, greed, hatred and delusion. When confused by fear, there is no possibility for clear seeing and cannot remember that compassion is the redemptive response. There is more than one potential available at any time. You can all speculate different outcomes for the abbot.

One-pointed, focused-concentration, causes fear, greed, anger and confusion to disappear. A wonderful focus I use is, "I am the wisdom of the natural deeper mind and all is revealed". The direct experience of the pleasure—indeed, the joy—of benevolence, over time, lessens the habitual self-centered, defensive actions of the mind and strengthens the habit of friendly acceptance. The responsive behavior—motivated by kindness—replaces reactive behavior. You become more peaceful and passionate person. At the soul level, you are one—not just a small piece of divine essence existing separately. Our connection to the Mind of God, Void, or Quantum is complete and seamless and in turn, loving relationship with the universe in totality.

This relates to frequency, again. Psycho-physiologists at Heart Math Institute have developed a method of modeling the fluctuating electromagnetic fields of the heart in response to emotion. The heart emits complex fields of energy that are directly affected by feelings. Emotions such as love actually make the energy fields more coherent (stronger), while emotions such as hatred and jealousy degrade the fields making them incoherent (weaker). As the coherent field of the heart expands through the emotion of love, it touches and enlivens other glands and organs of the body. Scientific research confirms that love is as dramatic and potent as medicine, both when it is present and when it is withdrawn.

Superimposing the energy field of fear upon a double helix structure shows the length of the low frequency waves allow few opportunities for the helix and wave to touch. The wave discourages access to the biological structure allowing its expression. This is the result of limiting and contracted fear.

Superimposing the energy field of love upon the double helix shows that the shorter length of high frequency waves allows more opportunities for the helix and wave to intersect. The wave encourages access to the helix. There are greater numbers of potential coding sites available due to the increased number of

You hear a lot about unconditional love, yet love itself has no conditions; it is a field of energy with emotional components.

Numerous things can stimulate it. Whether it is conditional or unconditional depends on the stimulus, with what people associate with love feelings, and the conditions they place upon giving and receiving love.

Redefining love as surrender to the mystery of our own spirit—our primary relationship, becomes a relationship with Self. Love comes when you show our soul to another. Surrender is to relinquish everything that deprives you of love and nurture everything that comes from love. How you feel affects your health! Lovingness has no boundaries and no specific recipients, timeless without space. It is a state of being or a condition of the mind, and as such is not specifically associated with an object nor with the heart; it is neither sexual, nor is it connected with a specific person. Lovingness is a quality of a coherent field that provides a happy awareness.

Christos, meaning To Know, is a key to power. Jesus Christ, the man Jesus, in Christos, his knowledge, in the image of God. (Jesus the Christ in knowledge of the Mind of God, his father, from whence all things come and his many kingdoms.) This is going to sound blasphemous, you, in knowledge of the

Mind of God and his many kingdoms. You acting on knowledge, in wholeness with all there is, can choose your kingdom.

In Sanskrit, to be in ecstasy permanently is liberation. Liberation or freedom means being born into fullness or wholeness, no separation. Esctasy means to step outside of the world of space, time, form and phenomena to experience unbinding into a world that is timeless.

I AM that which I Am becoming. We see we are being the experience of whatever we are experiencing with the ability to be equal.

Thou art That, shows us the sacred nature of the beloved; being both love and the lover.

All this is That, explands to encompass every particle in the universe. Instead of feeling separate, consider a feeling that "I" inhabit a body with infinite consciousness and it expands with infinite speed through infinite dimensions. Sound familiar.

Taking this a step further, love and spirit are the same force. That unseen force at the core of our being.

Love, as energy, can be shared with others. How? There are as many ways as there are people. Reaching out to hold a hand or touch a shoulder transfers this energy and felt by the recipient. Using kind and loving words can transfer this energy. Smiling at a stranger can lift a soul. Holding a door open can lighten a burden. When you use this love energy it produces a powerful result that others can feel your love and can be healed, and lifted.

A client had an experience with a former husband refusing to pay child support, ten years after the divorce. She was angry, felt betrayed, and thought it horrible that someone would not want to help support his child. As a single parent, she struggled for years financially to raise her son with good values, self-esteem and creativity. All the emotions flared again, just as if it happened yesterday. With Coaching, she remembered the other side of holding on to anger, betrayal and loss. That picture was not pretty. What he does with his life is his creation. He has his own beliefs and his own version. The alternative to anger, betrayal and loss, not to mention three years lost in court and attorney fees, finally, to see what love could do. It didn't take a saint to figure that one out. What could she possibly create with that kind of atmosphere? Did she get child support? No. The new vision allowed her to relax about the situation and let go...thus, the miracle could happen, she is no longer struggling and her son is on to quite an adventure. This was her ultimate dream, anyway.

Remember to relinquish that which deprives love, and nurture everything that comes from love. What IS important, is YOU and YOUR WELL-BEING.

Another client learned the lesson that no matter how much she did or grew, other people would have their opinions whether she changed or not. She learned she had nothing to fear in others opinions. She would live her life as she designed. Intimidation had no place in her new life. Insecurity had not place in her life.

The act of using love energy also is a powerful tool for your own self-care. Look at the face of someone who is open, loving and not protected. What does this type of person do? They are alive, happy, free, and you sense a joy for living. Love is a life force. To open your heart and be an expression of love, you have to be like a young child.

The world doesn't need changing; the world needs loving. Imagine there are six billion on the planet and most of them are afraid to pen their hearts and express love. Don't wait for someone else to make the first move. Take the first step and express love, even if you don't feel safe enough. This is just one example of how one person can make a grand shift. You then create your life where it is safe for others to open their hearts and express their love, one at a time.

Take the responsibility. Any relationship is not 50/50; it is 100/100. When you blame someone else, you may be telling the truth from your perspective, however, at the same time, you are giving your power away. You say that you are not responsible. When you are not responsible, there is nothing you can do. You make yourself a victim. To have your life be as great as it can be, give up the blaming and find your limitation. Then take whatever action you need to handle your situation. Change your thoughts and change your relationship.

When you love, life is wonderful. You are happy, alive and free. You feel better about yourself and everything around you. What would it be like to create with this type of energy? Wow!

Exercise:

Pocket of Love - Carry red and pink hearts in your pocket or pretend that you have them. Each day awaken with a pocket of love and give it all away. It is renewable each day. Love can be a word, tone of voice, joke, touch, pat on the back, encouragement, understanding or compassion. (See appendix 6 for some thoughts to ponder on love)

Okay, What's love got to do with getting what you want? You are the observer.

As long as you're going to think anyway—

Think BIG!
If you are going to manifest...
Love your creation.

When you often look at your goals and aspirations, they can often reflect an imagined future lifestyle in which everything is a lot different from the way you live now. It could be money, confidence, spare time, clothes, friends, partner, house, or car.

This is a clue. Many, future imagined lifestyles remain "head" dreams, false goals, or goals that exist entirely in the intellect, without passion or love.

In order to create you must incorporate desire, which is love. When you desire something, you love it. When you desire something, you feel love for it and you feel love for the relationship you could have with that something.

Can you desire something that bears absolutely no relation to our present life?

An example, you want a BMW. You have a desire for a BMW. Unless you have seen a BMW, had some experience of one, shown some appreciation for a BMW, ridden in one or at least had some sort of relationship with a BMW, how relevant could the goal be? The conclusion is that a owning a BMW is just a nice idea.

Relationship with what you want to manifest defines the genuineness of your desire and more importantly, your appreciation of things instills passion into these desires. Remember atmosphere? Appreciation naturally leads to desire. How often have you heard, I'd love to do it or have it?

This is **crucial** to understand for manifesting. When you experience love and appreciation it is within you; it's your love that feels great. In that moment that thing is your manifestation; you have it. Because you have it at that moment, energetically it is done. You are, therefore what you desire. The relationship is established and you are connected to our goal and action begins. Now there is a direction for life. Here is where the law of attraction begins to work.

In the Mind of God, Quantum or Void, this energetic desire meets with its end result. Circumstances start to happen, doors open, or someone shows up with the result. You can only experience what is reflected in the life and the attitude of the individual doing the desiring.

Remember atmosphere? If you are feeling anything less than love when you set out to bring forth your dreams and desires, the dream or desire will be tainted by your feelings, whether it be guilt, fear, anger, loss, or any negative emotion. The dream or desire will reflect the emotion that is set into motion with your vision.

No one guarantees the goals. There is no implied requirement that these goals be met. An individual can spend an entire lifetime professing to want happiness, strength, compassion and the list goes on, yet feel no requirement to do anything about having these things now. An individual can speak about these desires with passion and still no appreciation or relationship to the goal, it will not happen.

Love has everything to do with manifesting. A willingness to express a kind of appreciation or acknowledgment for what you have, a willingness to be allowing of others and having what you desire now, the goals for change are in your favor. The only way to commit to change in life is to make it a direction and to adopt a desire for more, educate yourself, take action and be prepared to embrace all that it entails.

You can now understand that Love is a sacred, motivating principle, which governs the Mind of God, quantum field or the void. Believe it or not, unseen or not—just as any other law of science, it works. Gravity is real in a 3D world, if you jump out a window you are going down. Love is a state of being not an emotion.

Love may be seen as a collapsing of the past and being free of the emotion of that past that limits us. Without limitation and the new wisdom; have the ability to see the actions of others without emotion or judgment. Recognize your experiences as what they are—without the involvement or drama of it. Sounds like the ability to do and create what you want; being in the world but not allowing its drama to influence your dreams and desires.

Whisper to me intimately like a lover for tenderness is rare in this world. It is difficult to convey the magic of love to those who are made of dust...Rumi

Chapter 8

Science and Miracles

Aquinas says a miracle is "beyond the order commonly observed
The Fierce Power of Imagination is a gift from God. Joined with the grandeur of the mind, the potency of inference, ethical depth, and natural sense of the divine, imagination becomes an instrument for the Holy Spirit.
...The Essential Kabala, Daniel Matt

What is a miracle? Webster's Dictionary describes it as "any occurrence that is not explainable by the laws of nature or an event that surpasses all known human or natural powers and is ascribed to divine or supernatural cause." A miracle is a supernaturally (divinely) caused event - an event (ordinarily) different from what would have occurred in the normal ("natural") course of events.

Is it possible to have a science of miracles? Perhaps if we look closer using the theories of quantum physics, we may see some similarities.

Another word, Shaman, has held great fascination for me ever since I first heard it. Shaman (Shah muhn) is described as a person considered to have powers that come from direct contact with the supernatural (beyond natural), often in dreams, trances or the void. Considering what we have learned about quantum foam, Mind of God, perhaps we are all potential Shamans.

You can explore Shamans from a quantum perspective. They have two things in common. First, They see the universe as made from vibrations. The second commonalty is they will use any device to change a patient's belief about his reality.

Let's say a 21st century hiker from Seattle enters the deep rainforest and observes a Shaman, covered in blood, wearing the skin of a wild animal and dancing wildly around a fire. The Shaman slowly moves to an injured tribesman, waves his arms, and chants. Then he pronounces the injured tribesman healed. The tribesman gets up and is healed. The hiker would think that was a miracle, not completely understanding the sciences of mind, consciousness, physics, biology and imagination.

And, if the Shaman happened upon the 21st century hiker from Seattle, who carried a laptop computer to monitor his stock portfolio or check emails, the Shaman would think that was a miracle. Images in a box that you can change, not understanding the science of computer transmission and generation.

Both the hiker and the Shaman see these experiences as a natural thing, each in their perspective worlds. Taken out of each element, it would appear as a miracle.

The word "Master," as in the Teachings of the Masters of the Far East, carried with it an imaginary, superhuman—state of Divinity that was awesome and apart from the attainment of ordinary human beings. The miracles of Jesus were tabulated as something that could occur at that period of history, and by Him alone, but were not linked with possibilities of modern times even though Jesus taught, "Greater things than these shall you do."

These have been presented with all sorts of mystery, translation and mistakes. Anything that appears mysterious or secret should be challenged by each of us. Through investigation, we become knowledgeable and can make better choices. Through the science of quantum mechanics and the nature and mind, we can discover the answers to the mysterious. There is no limit to the power of the human mind. The more concentrated it is, the more power is brought to a single point—that is the "secret" or the door to knowing. The more you understand, the more miracles can happen in your life.

There is a pre-physical shape of the body that is similar to an architect's blueprint of a house. The architect's mind has the picture of the house and knows how it will manifest and take form. Nature's architects don't have homeowners that change their minds half way through the process. Most of the time, Nature turns out objects of mutation with perfection.

Cleve Baxter, an early pioneer in lie detection, discovered an energy field around the body. He demonstrated that plants not only are sensitive to their surroundings but they can literally be identified and individual. For example in a mock trial, the killer of a plant was identified by another plant in the same room, at the time of the murder. The witness plant was hooked up to a lie detector. The witness plant was on the stand and the prosecution brought in a person who cared for the plants and no readings changed. He then brought a suspect of the murder into the room. The witness plant's readings were going crazy, thus identifying the killer through frequency readings.

There is a special photographic process called Kirlian Photography, where one can take a photo of anything and when developed, all around the edges of the object, you see a brilliant glow of various-colored light. This is the subtle field blueprint of the object. The blueprint remains for some time even after taking away a part of the object. This would explain "phantom limb" pain—even though a person had lost an arm or leg, they still feel as though it is there.

I met Stanford School of Medicine Cellular Biologist, Dr. Bruce Lipton, while attending a lecture in Yelm, WA. He told of an experiment where cells of the body were removed and transported to distances as much as five miles away from the host organ. Both were closely

95

monitored.   When one was traumatized, the
other responded sympathetically, regardless of
the distance.   One of your cells, five miles
away from you, can respond to its environment
and your body would respond.   This accounts
for   healing-at-a-distance,   knowing   what's
happening when you are away from home or an
eerie feeling at an intersection before you
witness an accident.

Dr.   Dean   Ornish,   a   San   Francisco
cardiologist, demonstrated that 40 patients
with advanced heart problems could actually
shrink the fatty plaque deposits that were
progressively   blocking   their   coronary
arteries.   Dr. Ornish had this group use
simple yoga exercises, meditation and a strict
low-cholesterol diet.

What is so astounding about this study is
that no mainstream medicine had ever before
acknowledged that heart disease could be
reversed once it has started.   The good news
about Ornish's study is that what you build in
your body, we can also rebuild.

The cells of you body can cooperate when
they develop an illness, giving one's mind an
alternative to having to face a situation it
could not (or did not want to) face.   For
example, a tummy ache to avoid school; loss of
a voice to avoid facing an audience; a heart
attack is socially acceptable, but not a
vacaton; and cancer in a woman to keep her
roving husband home and attentive.

Going back to the story of Eve, when the
arthritic personality was there, she could not
paint or play the piano.   When the other

personality was there, she could play the piano. Could the change in personality cause the cells to remember, and thus cause a change in physiology or wellness?

Somehow, did a hypnotic suggestion remove the psychological barriers that caused the dysfunction? Quantum physics state a particle can be a wave or a particle (light or solid). Matter can be particles, localized points in space; or it can be waves, energy dispersed over a finite volume.

Matter's total identity (quantum wave packet) includes potentialities for both forms—particles and waves. Subatomic particles are a coagulation of information (thought). Everything has a matrix (pattern that gives definition (destiny) to something (object). The observer defines if the wave is a wave or particle and collapses the wave function. It appears that Eve's different personalities, each, were the observer at the time of occupancy, which then dictated the physical state of the body.

Quantum mechanics tells us that pushing and swirling electrons produce specific blueprints, building molecules of many shapes and purpose. The word blueprint or matrix is used to describe for example, the creative process of a cloud or "wave packet." A wave packet holds information telling the atoms what to do.

In other words, the fields around the atom "feel" or "read" the environment and come back to the atom as information potentials. The atom then responds to the information received. Subatomic particles are the coagulation of a thought (information or packet).

Let's look at a representative drawing of the human energy form.

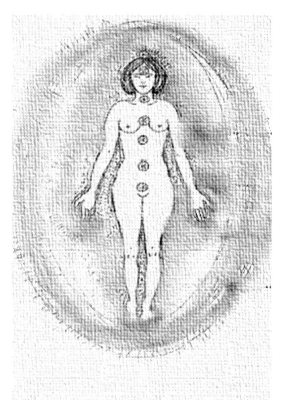

Human energy form, drawn to show electromagnetic spectrum surrounding the body and penetrating the body. Circular disks represent the energy centers.

This matrix or pattern of information gives definition (destiny) to the wavelengths. David Bohm, a British physicist proposed that there is an "invisible field" that holds all of reality together, a field that possesses the property of knowing what is happening everywhere at once. This is called the Mind of God, Void or quantum.   Our bodies each have a matrix and as John Lilly once stated, we are all swimming in a giant ocean.   Some call the matrix around the body, an aura, or the electro-magnetic bands (bio-energy field around the body) or just **the mind of** Joe, Camille, Millie, or Robert.

This energy field not only goes around you, but moves within your body as well.   It is not just the outside of your body that is made of electromagnetic energies. Every part of your body is permeated and everything you experience is the electromagnetic spectrum. These bands vibrate to different color, sound and light frequency, and according to the physical, emotional, mental and spiritual states, this energy field can shift (remember atmosphere).

This field has been validated in scientific laboratories as light emissions using photometers and color filters, as Dr Valerie Hunt describes in her book, *Infinite Mind*. Each of these bands is harmonically related and has its unique atmosphere, frequency, and information.

Your physical body is the densest of these bands or bodies that use consciousness of the others to explore its environment and interact with others through its senses of touch, taste, smell, sight and feeling.   You see, then that our physical body is really a field of vibrating energy that has coagulated from a higher frequency or octave.

As human beings we are both living magnets and power sources of human energy.   You radiate our unique energy and attract into your life those people and circumstances that are in tune with your unique thoughts.

Science demonstrates the electromagnetic spectrum as:

Electromagnetic Spectrum

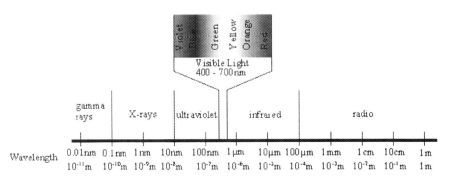

Quantum theory tells us that in the realm of the ultramicroscopic there is dimensions curled up each upon itself, so miniscule, they have been undetected, until now. There are six dimensions shown here, science has no scientific name for what exists beyond these six other than ether. Quantum theory calls it the quantum; unknown void.

We can twist along through dimensions of the Electromagnetic Spectrum into a circular, multilevel matrix it would look similar to the human energy form, above. Actually, everything has this energy form around it.

Waves begin from the Void, Quantum, Mind of God, and follow along the levels of the spectrum, which suggests an emergence from a preexistent level of manifestation. This reveals the limitless light emanating throughout our universe. Moving through the electromagnetic spectrum from the void, to gamma rays, x-ray, ultra violet, white light, infrared and then to hertzian.

The initial level radiates from the void at wavelengths equivalent to nuclear particles. Cellular processes on the biological level organize at dimensions identical to light waves. Evolution presently occurring in our genetic code is due to the exposure of delicate DNA strands to disruptive Ultra Violet wavelengths and our thought processes. Infra Red light waves are radiated from warm living organisms, with waves well within the size of individual cells. The size range of Visible Light is reflected with the human chromosomes.

Seeing the Electromagnetic Spectrum in this manner reinforces the basis for using the dimensional levels of organization. Energy Rays, Light Waves, and Sound Waves each have equal parts, which correspond to a specific range of physical manifestation. This is a more comprehensive view of the spectrum, where each level is built upon the one that precedes it.

Quantum Theory also tells us the observer defines the action by collapsing the wave function.

When you, as observer, think; you influence the field of potential energy into particles. With focused awareness, you can change the spin of an atom. Depending on where your own vibrational level of consciousness is at any given time, there are different effects. Remember the emotional, chemical, electrical signatures of energy.

The quantum uses your thoughts, your mental images, as the instruction to create your reality in the material world. To express means to make known, state, communicate or convey. This force does not know which of your thoughts to manifest into experience and which not to. That's why it is imperative to be clear in what you desire, have a lot of information, passion and certitude to manifest just what you want in an experience. They are paramount to manifesting exactly what you desire. Any of these ingredients missing, and the desire is manifested differently.

This reminds me when a client slipped on wet clay while descending a hill, with an ax following closely behind, which she refused to let go. It was borrowed and she had to return it. She fractured a rib, tore ligaments in her neck and arm, and had a serious case of neuralgia from the neck through the right arm.

Ripping feelings tugged at the shoulder, twisting muscle pain in the upper arm with pins and needles in the lower arm, left her weak. Occasionally, the arm was numbed and inaccessible. Sleeping was nearly impossible, except for small naps. After three weeks of pain treatment, there was no relief. She incorporated guided imagery in a self-described powerful meditative state, seeing the arm and shoulder healed, new nerves and full use of the entire body dancing, my favorite hobby. Her focused attention and joy were so powerful she knew she was healed. For the next two days, there was no pain, pins and needles or numbness.

Within a few days, she returned to the doctor and explained her experience. She was told that the body had improved yet more work was still needed to mend. She returned home only to discover the pain had returned. Immediately, she returned to her focus of dancing with a fully functioning body in joy. Then, the pain subsided. Holding the vision as real allowed her body is to grow into the new matrix or blueprint of well-being. The subjective reality and objective reality are tightly bound together. When the mind shifts, the body cannot help but follow.

After learning about quantum physics, belief, certitude and the way the brain works with emotion, you begin to see that miracles can be quite common. That's magic! Change the image and you change your reality! You can replace struggle, fear and uncertainty with the memory of health; patients experienced spontaneous regression of their diseases. Remember our floodgates of molecules of emotion, cell receptor sites and new tissue.

The doctor may have assumed what is "in her head" is not real or at least very inferior to the reality of the condition.

Being trained in scientific methods, he knew the predictable outcomes of various kinds of conditions. He tried to push it back into the range of predictable. Medical statistics appeal to the head. She held her ground and continued to focus on her reality, with treatments and recovered at a quicker rate. Remember, she was not in denial of the situation and doing nothing. She became the observer in the quantum world and created her desired intent with certitude.

The fear in a doctor's eyes or voice can strike of condemnation. One may hear, "you are definitely going to recover," yet interpret it as, "you may recover if it wasn't so bad." One extreme, his reassuring words if believed, may be enough to make the difference in the patient's case. The other extreme, if he actually thinks the patient is doomed, something in his voice will give that message, and from it a destructive confusion may set in.

Anything can serve as a placebo. A doctor's bedside manner, antiseptic smell of hospitals, sugar pills or kind words—do not harm or do good; as much as it is the patient's interpretation of it. It's a process where psychological factors such as beliefs and expectations trigger a healthy healing response that can be as powerful as any conventional therapy, be it drugs, surgery, or psychotherapy. Understanding the chemistry of the brain and emotions add to the theory of placebo. A placebo or nocebo component is present in all therapeutic interactions. If one believes surgery will cure the problem, it can, or if one doubts the therapist's capability or the treatment, a nocebo one takes place.

Physics tells us the point of zero vibration is not an empty vacuum of a void, but the starting point for everything that exists. This starting point is always in contact with every other point—there are no breaks in continuity. We experience this subatomic void every time we think. When we have a thought— "I am happy." a chemical messenger translates the emotion, having no solid existence whatever in the material world, into a bit of matter so perfectly attuned to the desire, that literally every cell in the body learns of the happiness and joins in. What really is created out of nowhere is the configurations of what thought is.

Objective reality looks obviously more fixed than our subjective moods, fleeting desires and swings of emotion. Perhaps, it is like playing a violin, you can hold one pitch but also change pitch as your finger slides along the string. The pitch demonstrates the level of consciousness. It is very difficult to think yourself into a different pitch (level of consciousness). This helps to explain that meditation, focused attention, and imagery is not simply another kind of thinking.

It is a way to slide to a new pitch; change harmonics, and transcend...go beyond.

To undo a particular ailment in the body, you must move from one pitch that is out of tune to a more harmonious pitch. You could use focused attention to create a picture holographically in the brain in which this genius transmits as energy and information packets (waves) to the body to change the matrix (blueprint) of the disease to health (pitch). To change the energy (pitch), collapse the wave function and build a new matrix of health.

In other words, awareness takes thought away from the physical disease long enough to liquefy (relax and unwind particles back to a wave), then uses the brain in willful focus to create a holographic picture (new matrix or blueprint) to collapse the wave function and coagulate around the new matrix (blueprint) to form an entirely different form (health). If you project the same image everyday, your reality will be the same everyday.

This field of intelligence is extremely sensitive to change, however both for good and ill. This communication network is on 24/7. It never sleeps.

When working with a gentleman with prostate cancer, he was able to see the relationship with his concept of healing the cancer opposed to the doctor's expectations, his pain, anger, helplessness, fear and delusion. His noticed his whole concept of self had changed everything in his life. Through the work we did, he overcame these obstacles and created a healthier body. He learned about the science behind the miracle he expected. With clarity, attitude, focus and certitude, he changed his nutrition, his thought processes, and had time to travel, enjoyed his wife, and indulged in pampering himself.

Dr. Ellen Langer, in an article entitled, *Reversing the Clock;* described her research project reversing certain characteristics of aging. Basically she had taken "old people" out of their environment and exposed them to photographs, music, and discussions that were current twenty years earlier. The result was the group became younger looking by three years, biological age was 12 years younger than the chronological age in years, gained weight, behaved more independently and could actually hear and see better.

Miracles occur just by remembering. When remembering, the brain thinks it is happening NOW in time and releases the same chemicals as the remembered scene.

Nature is full of miracles. The metamorphous of the caterpillar into the butterfly is a great analogy. Perhaps we can learn to imitate the caterpillar, get rid of that cocoon of mistakes and non-productive beliefs and fly.

Metamorphous of the Caterpillar is nature's greatest example

As the Caterpillar: DNA makes segments of a caterpillar chain reaction amino acids, RNA

As the chrysalis/cocoon: DNA liquefies, 9 segments harmonically to dissolving cell structure backward to protein, to DNA-molecules-atomic acids.

The Dream (potential mind of butterfly) harmonically, reforms to a new structure.

When we use our ability to visualize or imagine, we close ourselves within a cocoon. We close out all of the known senses, beliefs, and relax into the world of the quantum to create the desired change. The butterfly is considered a miracle of nature. Let's see how we can now use the knowledge gained and our brains to create our desires and more miracles.

Chapter 9

Dimensionality and the Grand Architect

Look to your experience and ask, "Who is it that is always witnessing or observing my mind? Who is it that is always watching? The answer, "I am."

Many Hall

Understanding and aligning yourself with the natural principles that govern the workings of our universe, our mind, brain, body and learning to use these principles in the most conscious and creative way—creates miracles.

We all know how information travels on a radio wave. Take a specific wave of electromagnetic energy at a specific frequency and then modulate the amplitude of that wave or the frequency.

That gives us amplitude modulation (AM) and frequency modulation (FM) radio. A song rides along with the radio wave, kind of like a surfer following a swell. The song's message, "love is all there is" is the same at both sending and receiving stations. The only flaw is, the information is tied to the radio wave, and it is limited to the distance that the radio wave can travel.

In actuality, within the cerebral cortex reside the estimated 10 billion neurons linked by 1 million billion connections. If we would count these connections at the rate of one connection per second, it would take **32 million years** to complete. Even a section of the brain no bigger than a match head contains about a billion connections. Consider that the number of positively charged particles in the whole known universe is only ten followed by 80 zeros (10,000,000,000,000,000,000,000,000,000,000,000,000,000,000,000,000,000, etc.). These neurons communicate in combination of electricity and chemistry (neurotransmitters).

To begin to imagine 10 billion and one neurons firing, perhaps we could look at the analogy in the computer world—the World Wide Web. If you could imagine a 3-D version of the hook-ups of the World Wide Web, superimposed over the picture of the United States. There would be a number of main trunks across the top, intersecting at various points. Next, would be smaller trunks to connect a network of smaller trunk that connects to telephone nodules that connect telephone lines to individual computers.

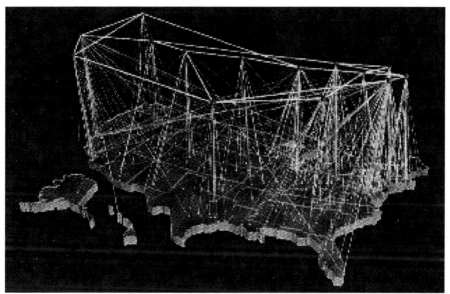

In one particular system, one person with a personal computer at home in Olympia can call a local number and reach a library system in Olympia, which connects through a carrier to the World Wide Web (Internet) via Seattle or Portland. This in turn is connected to Los Angeles or Phoenix, then to Provo, Utah. It can then go to New York. From New York it can go to most anywhere, just to connect to a critique group at MIT. One thing about the Internet World Wide Web is that it is random. Sitting in Olympia, the call may lead to Seattle or Portland and from there it is random to other places, and so on. No one owns the World Wide Web—yet.

You can reach any destination anywhere, while sitting in Olympia.

Our brains are capable of the same thing. With the firing of so many neurons sitting in Olympia, we can effect and affect other brains sitting in Olympia, Seattle, Portland, New York or Japan.

Once we begin to see we are oscillating frequencies intermingling with other oscillating frequencies, we may begin to notice our influence on our own bodies and others. We can influence the cell with consciousness to heal itself, to grow anew or regenerate. In this world, nothing is static; instead is ever in flux, mutable. How powerful are we as humans with information that is applied in our lives?

In quantum physics, Heisenberg's Uncertainty Principle if you measure the light as a particle then it behaves like a billiard ball when struck by another, and gets pushed around. If you measure light as a wave, then it behaves like the tides at the beach in which a floating log will move up and down as the wave passes through, but not forward. In Quantum Theory, light is not determined to be a particle or a wave until the moment it is observed or given definition by thought. The reason why both can exist in one reality is that they preexist as mere possibilities in the quantum field. The act of observation causes the potentiality of the wave packet to "collapse" into one aspect. Thus, one potential becomes enacted, while the others instantly disappear; but are not lost; (Worlds within Worlds, or wheel within a wheel or parallel universes). No longer can we study anything as separate from ourselves. Our acts of observation are part of the process that brings forth the manifestation of what we are observing. Particles remain as fuzzy bundles until they are observed. Only then do they become a thing. (At the moment the wave packet collapses, quantum phenomena give way and Newtonian physics reenters the picture.)

The brain translates consciousness, as coded wave patterns, into the coherent state we call human mind. Here's an example of the difference between interference patterns and a cohesive image. Consider a pianist playing Chopin. Where is the music? You can find it at many levels - in the vibrating strings, the trip of the hammers, the fingers striking the keys, the black marks on the paper, or the nerve impulses produced in the player's brain. But all of these are just codes; the reality of music is the shimmering, beautiful, invisible form that which haunts our memories without ever being present in the physical world.

Like a computer that translates electric impulses as on and off signals. These impulses are translated into bits, the bits into bytes and the bytes into the patterns of language that produce a program. A stimulated brain is richer in synaptic potential, thus able to process more code. It is more like having a 3 gig Pentium as opposed to an 8 bit 286. Not only is the quantity of information processing greater, with the capability of more sophisticated programming, or waveform transformation; the quality is also greater.

John Bell, physicist, constructed mathematical proof to show such a thing as "instantaneous action-at-a-distance" could occur in the universe. He demonstrated that the properties influenced by two particles can form a whole together, yet be apart in space and at the same time be connected, while traveling at light speed in opposite directions. The theory of non-locality was proven by Alain Aspect; a French physicist in 1982. An x particle here and a y particle anywhere can experience the same information instantaneously.

Energy expresses itself by molding itself around the information (thought) and becomes a particle. These particles then coagulate and form a matrix (blueprint) then, continues to fill in and creates matter. Cells affect other cells at a distance, telepathy, instant healings, spontaneous regeneration, are they beginning to sound familiar? If light can send information across the universe in a split second, could we do that as well?

Thought and matter are only flip sides or different aspects of the same process. Look at it as dimensions of encoded messages. Thought reflected in the quantum is the organizing aspect of this sea of virtual possibilities. Thought is frozen codes being translated at a certain frequency. Yet the virtual possibilities, within this sea of everything, are vibrating at many levels. Everything is possible, but only one thing is happening right now, right here.

Our brain can be seen as a probability organizer. It moves possibilities into probabilities. It translates one of many frequencies into reality.

Quantum physics, tells us that we create our own reality as we go, the universe is very

uncertain (be happy or eat desert first).
Everything is possible, but not probable. You
are each living in a parallel world of our own
and everything is made up of light waves
interfering with one another.

Sounds a little bit like Holographic
pictures doesn't it. By interfering two or
more laser beams, you can make a picture
appear that looks very real, but is like a
ghost. What gives the ghost the definition?
Consciousness. If consciousness is thought,
then consciousness enacting on a brain can
cause physiological change. Remember the
lemon? You are what you think, right now...
and now...and now. You put the environment in
which you worry about there. If you
acknowledge the role you play in this
creation, it changes the things you talk and
argue about. If you create the environment,
how can you argue about its objective
features, or about what's true or false? You
did it!

Physicist David Bohm's idea that there is an
explicate order and implicate order states:
The explicate order is the world as we're
typically perceiving it: full of objects with
apparent differences and boundaries. The
implicate order is the unbroken wholeness that
connects us all; it is the quantum level where
objects, and particles, and people, and
emotions are made, sub-atomically, of the same
substance.

On the explicate level, the observer and
that which is observed (thoughts, emotions,
sensations) appear to be different. On the
implicate level, they are one and the same.

Let's say - in the mind of Jill—she has a thought of a cake. She gathers all the ingredients -the flour, butter, sugar, vanilla, eggs, etc. and changes the level of energy through heating things up (baking). This process of gathering and blending is the implicate order and the explicate order is the result the thing called cake. Now in the mind of Jill's cake, is the all and all which still holds the properties of the flour, butter, sugar, vanilla, eggs, etc. They did not disappear; they changed their atmosphere, energy and information. Now the mind of Jill and the mind of cake have a relationship within the mind of God or quantum void. It makes no difference in the level of the creation whether it's a cake, wealth, or wellness.

Baird T. Spalding, in his Life and Teaching of the Masters of the Far East, Volume 6, told of incidence that was photographed.

He stated that a porter fell asleep on a boat, about ten o'clock and his hand dropped into the water. A crocodile snapped it off. The man jumped ashore and appealed to one individual and walked toward him, a master. By the time he had gotten face to face with this individual, the photographs show that the pain had left and that the blood had stopped flowing. Successive photographs were taken for the next forty-five minutes; during the last eight minutes, every photograph showed the hand complete. By two o'clock in the afternoon the man returned to his place in the boat. While every white man showed wonderment. Not one native did. They all accepted it. To the natives, it was a common thought that such could happen. It was not a miracle. It was expected to happen—that's certitude.

Certitude is an essential ingredient in the mix of manifestation of dreams. Certitude, as Webster puts it: The state of being certain; complete assurance; confidence. **2.** Sureness of occurrence or result; inevitability. **3.** Something that is assured or unfailing.

I was diagnosed with cancer of the thyroid and pituitary. I experienced lethargy, mood swings, weight gain, severe headaches and loss of concentration. Not accepting the picture of the diagnosis, I knew I was more than the physical body, alone. Through meditation and questioning myself, I discovered my body was adapting due to anger that stemmed from not expressing myself creatively. I felt trapped by circumstances. My desires were not being met sufficiently, if at all. With the help of a healing group, I practiced focused-willful imagery and dynamic meditation along with audiotapes for reinforcing my new body structure of health and positive thinking. Totally positive in my belief to heal myself, I started feeling better. Within three weeks all symptoms were completely gone. Reluctantly, I returned for further testing to find no traces of cancer and no sign that any had ever been present. It was a miracle? Spontaneous Regeneration, said the physician.

Consciousness is more pervasive than medicine gives it credit. Even when it is ignored the void, Mind of God or Quantum—that grand intelligence, knows what is happening. Its knowledge reaches beyond buffers and screens, going farther than we expect. The observer in us is capable and has the power to reveal what is hidden and what is needed.

The brain is also capable of making wave packets or scalar waves. Each side of the brain is emitting electromagnetic frequencies that can be measured by an EEG (electroencephalograph). If you can learn to get both sides of your brain turned on with equal intensity and at the same frequency, you could do many miracles. There are a number of methods of training to accomplish this: meditation, focused-attention, biofeedback, guided imagery, imagination, and workshops.

An information or wave packet in quanta can be understood equally well by the person writing this book, as the person reading the book, provided your brain is up to par (the integrity of the receiver).

Dr. Bob Beck, biologist, discovered that psychics, healers, and Kahunas, while doing their 'magic' moved to the brain wave frequency of 7.83 Hz. and miracles occurred. I teach people how to do this with the help of relaxation and meditation practices. They were able to do many things that were outside of normal experience. For example, reduce tumors, increase or decrease blood flow, reprogram attitudes, seeing things at a distance (remote view), healed faster with less complications, relax, become more confident in their own abilities. Bob Beck was asked not to continue this research, something to do with national security.

As a tool, I researched sound to induce brain hemispheric synchronization. Using binaural beats—a signal in one ear, e.g. 100 Hz. And another signal in the other ear slightly different, say 108 Hz., the brain then produced an 8 Hz. signal. It has been found that if you pulse a tone at 4 Hz or four cycles per second, brain activity will tend to move toward that window of entrainment, the threshold between Theta and Delta. If you pulse the same tone at 8 Hz, the brain will tend to entrain itself more to the Alpha range of activity. It is now possible to be a kind of electronic shaman, creating tonal patterns that entrain the brain towards windows of brain wave activity. Our research demonstrated this to be very effective.

The key is to alter the brain state, enter the more relaxed areas of Alpha and/or Theta, and then set up a protocol in which one would "act as if"—what you experience is real. Under the right conditions, it is possible to affect changes in the physical body through changes in mental and emotional experience.

Results of a study entitled, "*REST and Creativity Enhancement*," published in the *2nd International Conference on REST Proceedings*, 1987, by Dr. Baker:

1. Ability to relax   90%

2. Stopping Internal Dialog   70%

3. Ability to Reduce Discomfort   70%

4. Ability to Concentrate   70%

5. Increased Energy Levels   70%

6. Dreamlike State   70%

7. Ability to Receive Answers as a Workable

Solution   70%

The use of this experiential psychotherapeutic tool to reduce anxiety levels, reach deep-seated levels, exploring the stimulation of the immune system, increasing white cell count, dissolving tumors, and dealing with fear, anger and death among cancer patients and their families. (See appendix 5 for some comments from the medical field from using these tapes)

The clients entered a state of deep relaxation, marked by slower breathing and heartbeat, by the appearance of alpha waves in the EEGs (electroencephalogram) and decreased oxygen consumption detected in the breath.

They achieved deep relaxation with 5-10 minutes. Normally it takes four to six hours of sleep to reach this level of relaxation. This showed that the subjective feelings reported during these exercises -inner silence, peacefulness, relaxation, and connection - had a real physical basis. They were fully awake inside, and some had a sense of heightened awareness – not asleep or in a trance.

Again, the subjective reality and objective reality are rightly bound together. More information and dimensionality allows the brain more to model the next experience. Let's see what the brain states, relaxation and meditation have to do with it all.

Chapter 10

Physics and Brain States

One of the greatest scientific achievements imaginable would be the discovery of an explicit relationship between the waveform alphabets of quantum theory and certain human states of consciousness."
Nick Herbert, *QUANTUM REALITY*

Thought has also been defined as an image making process based on memory. Think of a television image or movie. It is made of images flashing rapidly to give the appearance of a person walking across the scene. In reality, it's only a film reel with 24 fames to the second, so your eyes do not detect the gap between the frames. Billions of light photons flashing at the speed of light like our reality at the quantum. This causes an illusion of being solid and continuous.

Resonating frequencies are primary physical bonds in nature.
For every frequency or frequency band there exists natural or created resonators. E.g. a

field's frequency pattern at any given time is a resonating structure that determines the energy it will absorb or will be affected. Each material substance, living or inert, mineral or chemical, has its own vibratory signature carried in the structure of its field.

The electromagnetic signature of what is most commonly meant by thought, appears at or around 15-16 Hz. Attention's electromagnetic signature, begins at 13-14 Hz, and includes frequencies that are in the Alpha range and Theta range.

An Electroencephalogram or EEG is the device to measure such brain activity. Brain waves are the resulting measurements. At any given moment there are thousands of different energy states occurring with brain stimulation. Some are biochemical, electro magnetic or some we do not even know about yet. Each thought, feeling, sight, touch, taste, sound has its own corresponding brain state or electromagnetic and biochemical matrix.

Generally speaking, neurologists use eight categories to divide brain waves. One Hertz (Hz) stands for 1 cycle per second (cps).

Super High Beta	35 -	150 Hz
K-complex	33 -	35 Hz
High Beta	18 -	32 Hz
SMR	15 -	17 Hz
Beta	12 -	15 Hz
Alpha	8 -	12 Hz
Theta	4 -	8 Hz
Delta	0.5-	4 Hz

Delta is that state where science describes there is the least amount of energy within the brain. It is the domain of sleep, usually no mental images and no awareness of the physical body. Although some seasoned people who meditate can experience a different state of being asleep, yet fully conscious.

In **Theta**, the neurons transduce energy at a faster rate than Delta. There may be little or no sense of the physical body, a sensation of floating or being unconnected. This is an inner state and the external reality is simply not experienced. It's the ideal state for some types of accelerating learning, self-programming and psycho-immunity (self healing). Daydreaming, dreaming, creativity, meditation, hypnosis, paranormal phenomena, effective prayer, out of body experiences, ESP and shamanism journeys are a few characteristics.

Ever driven a few miles and can't recall the last five miles or lost time in the shower, shaving or brushing your hair? It is a state where tasks become so automatic that you can mentally disengage from them. The ideation that can take place during the theta state is often free flow and occurs without censorship or guilt. It is typically a very positive mental state.

Professor Owen Flanagan of Duke University in North Carolina stated we can now hypothesize with some confidence that those apparently happy, calm Buddhist souls one regularly come across in places such as Dharamsala, India, really are Happy.

Paul Ekman of the University of California, San Francisco Medical Center suggests that mediation and mindfulness can tame the amaygdala, an area of the brain, which is the hub of fear memory.

Next is **Alpha**. This state is a kind of body asleep and mind awake. Also, it's a great state for accelerate learning (Lozanov's method of Superlearning), reducing the stress around learning. Relaxation times, non-arousal, meditation, and hypnosis are characteristics.

Beta is characterized as a high state of alertness or our normal waking state. The awaking awareness, extroversion, concentration, logical thinking or an active conversation are characterizations of this state. A person making a speech, a teacher or a talk show host would all be in beta when they are engaged in their work.

SMR stands for Sensory Motor Response. Joel F. Lubar, Ph.D. and Judith Lubar, M.S., L.C.S.W., from the University of Tennessee, have discovered that persons with attention deficit disorder (ADD) are generally unable to generate Beta activity when trying to focus on a task. ADD individuals find it difficult to stick with tasks, such as studying or following directions and flit like moths from one thing to another

High Beta is a state of even greater alertness and may relate to some states of anxiety. Super high Beta is just now being research. Most EEG equipment does not go beyond 35-40 Hz.

K-complex usually occurs in short bursts. There is much speculation and some feel it is the state of the "ah-ha" experiences of high creativity.

Valerie Hunt, Ph.D. has documented that the brain goes up to at least 150 Hz. Some reports indicate Super High Beta states produce phenomena such as "out of body experience," Kundalini releases (powerful energy flows up the central nervous system) and other dynamic psycho-spiritual states.

There is also a high order of images from the brain that are archetypal or holographic in nature when the brain cells are reflecting or allowing frequencies to pass through. These frequencies that are being emitted appear to be in the Alpha-Theta range. Carl Jung studied the phenomena and referred to the occurrence as "synchronicity".

When you "take charge" successfully, there is an increase in self-esteem and something referred to as knowing your control over your own experiences and behavior. Research has shown that people have their own unique brain state profiles. No two people are exactly alike in how their brains process brain wave patterns.

The ability to change your own brain state at will is a powerful resource. It allows you to accelerate your brain/mind's hidden potential and open worlds you may never have imagined existed. You can tap into that quantum foam, void, or the Mind of God and

Deborah Baker-Receniello, PhD, CLSC

translate the codes by vibrating at the same frequency.

Lester Fehmi, director of the Princeton Behavioral Medicine and Biofeedback Clinic states, we spend a lot of time desynchronized: narrow-focusing, objectifying, gripping...We haven't had in our culture a normalizing model, large amplitude, in-phase synchrony is the perfect place for rapid normalization. It's the place to go to for rapid healing and normalization of functions (alpha/theta).

British physicist C. Maxwell Cade, used an EEG device called the Mind Mirror to study 4,000 people and discovered they could develop in mental self-regulation—with symmetry of hemispheres and lucid awareness. Cade believes that the higher mind, on the neuropsychological level, was what Carl Jung called transcendent function and that it is manifested by the integration of left and right hemisphere synchrony through the reciprocal transmission of nervous impulses across the corpus callosum, the great bridge of nervous tissue which unites the two halves of the brain.

This would provide the union of conscious with unconscious mental contents, also known as analogical thinking or being. This would show the integration of the left hemisphere's extroverted, verbal, rational and abstract processes with the right hemisphere's introverted, visual-spatial, synthetic and holistic processes, also known as analogical mind.

Many clients reported reaching a level where they were quickly able to learn how to enter this state in the everyday lives, like the training-wheels effect. Each client felt as if their mind had reached a higher level of integration, with accompanying increases in mental powers and an unmistakable reorientation toward life. Some reported bursts of creativity, euphoria, and mystical feelings of being at one with the universe.

Neuroscientist Jerry Levy, of the University of Chicago once stated, "Great men and women of history did not merely have superior intellectual capacities with each hemisphere. They had phenomenal levels of emotional commitment, motivation, attention capacity—all of which reflected the highly integrated brain in action."

That state that all highly talented people are in, when they are doing what they do best and working at his highest level, whether it's mathematics, playing basketball, dancing, meditating, the perfect or peak experience—is all this just other words for "flow," "zone"— really the state of whole-brain integration through symmetry and synchronization; analogical mind. Many people immediately recognized this as a state they have experienced naturally.

A truly great performer is able to enliven the music through the sheer intention of their consciousness. This performer intuitively expresses into the music essential forms of human emotion and desire. Such waveforms cannot be captured on sheet music. They emerge from the spirit or consciousness of the performer.

Using your imagination and meditation are tools to change your consciousness—you are doing everything. It enhances or accelerates your ability to learn to enter different brain states and give you a positive reinforcement that something indeed is taking place and changing.

Candace Pert, NIMH neuroscientist stated that the brain is just a wet little mini-receiver of collective reality; A radio, that can be tuned to any frequency. The question is what programs do we want to hear? What programs are we capable of hearing? What programs are possible?

In Valerie Hunt's, *Infinite Mind*, she describes Pert's work as the direct interface between the mind-field and the bio-healing response. The neuropeptide communication system, a field telemetry system, "talks" most rapidly directly from cell to cell and from remote to local areas eliciting total cooperation.

This system not only integrates the lower bioprocess, but it has the exclusive communication lines between the mind-field and the senses, to instruct the healing process of the body as a whole, and local tissue in particular. In other words, the neuropeptide is the receiver and encoder; while the source of information can come slowly through the liquid system, it is rapid through the electromagnetic field. The energy field system is non-linear because it has no central clearing house or hierarchy like that of the brain to the body or a cell to a cell.

One of the most profound effects of imagination and meditation, in my own experience, has been the ability to reach the state of active watchfulness or focused attention—The Observer. To be able to watch your own thoughts and how they affect your brain wave frequency and amplitude, your ability to think clearly, and how some thoughts hinder that process and can cause inaction or inappropriate action.

The constant play of electrochemical activity across the brain can be related to active information in the quantum potential whereby the form of the whole determines the motion of individual parts. You can also see how a complex intention is generated within the brain and unfolds into complex thoughts and muscular actions. The brain extends through the entire nervous system. Just as troublesome thoughts and feelings can give rise to body tensions, so too certain attitudes and thoughts may unfold out of muscular disposition of the whole body.

If you look at strange attractors in physics not as something that destroys order but pictured as the global distribution of very subtle information, you see that the brain's activity could be controlled by an extremely subtle level of information. Thought is the response to that information in the form of folding and unfolding of electrochemical activity across the brain. Yet, behind the thought there may lie something that is infinitely faster and more subtle in its nature. The evidence from various meditation experiences suggests that indeed something deeper lies beyond thought and that the brain's capabilities are far greater than anyone suspects.

Memory can now be seen as non-local with specific thoughts unfolding out of a gentle action within the brain. When the brain is damaged locally or widely peppered, memory cannot be identified with any particular localized structure. There are structures in the hippocampus associated with the functioning of memory, but they seem to have more to do with how memory is processed, stored and retrieved than with its actual location.

F. David Peat, author of *Synchronicity: The Bridge Between Matter and Mind,* stated that the idea has already been proposed, with regard to the brain, that chaos is an order of such high degree of complexity that it lies beyond any simple description and requires a global map of infinite detail—a strange attractor. Chaos is usually the door through which one structure leaves and another enters—an opportunity for evolution. To make changes, one would not remain outside as controller, but would have to enter into the system directly and change the quality of its movement at the source of its actual generation. Neural nets can be taught to do new tasks and recognize patterns where data that is passing through the neural nets influences the sensitivity of each interconnection. Learning by modifying their interconnections.

Electro-medical researchers believe that each disease or functional disturbance has its own energy field, which must be reversed before healing can take place. Illness is seen as a disturbance first in the energy field and healing is the restoration of that field to health. Spiritual and psychic healers, on the other hand, place primary emphasis upon healing the soul when it gets off tract. They believe the source of an illness is forgetting who we are. They believe that outer healing saves the biological life, while inner healing focuses on belief systems as the contaminating source.

Fifteen years of research with the SE-5 Spectrum analyzer has demonstrated that field disturbance precedes all tissue changes.

Perhaps then, health should be viewed as the perfection and maintenance of a dynamic energy field, which is flowing, coherent, and strong, giving the capacity to interact through vibrations.

A new electromagnetic model of illness and health can be seen as the material tissue ages, gets sick and diseased. It repairs itself, but eventually entropy takes over and causes deterioration and disintegration. In the human field, with new energy introduction, the field improves or even becomes more refined. The field is affected before we breathe, eat, or ingest substances, making it the first line of disturbance, defense and regeneration. Regeneration comes from re-energizing the field, and hence the tissue.

Becker explains the regeneration process by cell dedifferentiation followed by redifferentiation. Dedifferentiation of cells means that a blood cell can loose its unique capacity to generate a blood cell and can be redifferentiation or transposition into a muscle cell, a nerve cell or a connective tissue cell. He believes that the magnetic energy flowing outward from the site of injury stimulates this.

The dedifferentiated cell accumulates around the injury and later become osteoblasts (bone creators), neuroblasts (nerve creators), and fibroblasts (creating patching or scar tissue).

Here the energy field can take over and operate like the nervous system when it is defective.

The informational field is responsible for the matrix of growth. The DNA is known to carry genetic information about cellular development. Material tissue can be destroyed, but a field cannot. Like a hologram, the field carries information, which guides development and regeneration.

Remember Hippocrates, "Disease is not an entity but a fluctuating condition of the patient's body—a battle between the substances of disease and the natural, self-healing tendency of the body." You can now understand the healing process, resembling a communication system between mind and matter with the energy field as the means of communication.

Looking at Meditation, Imagination and Brain States you find science verifying eastern

theory.   Scientist   Andrew   Newberg,   a
radiologist at the University of Pennsylvania,
investigating the effect of meditative state
on Buddhist monk's brains have found that
portions of the organ previously active become
quiet,   whilst   pacified   areas   become
stimulated.

They noticed a notable decrease in activity
in the back part of the brain, which
reinforced   the   general   suggestion   that
meditation leads to lack of spatial awareness
(no time/no space). There was an increase in
activity in the front part of the brain, the
area activated when anyone focuses attention
on a particular task (focused intentional
will, imagery).

The complex interaction between different
areas of the brain also resembles the pattern
of activity that occurs during other spiritual
or mystical experiences. Dr. Newberg found
that the Franciscan nuns activate the
attention area of the brain and diminished
activity in the orientation area. Dr. Newberg
state, when someone has a mystical experience,
they perceive that sense of reality to be far
greater and far clearer than your usual
everyday sense of reality.

In his book, *Why God Won't Go Away,* Andrew
Newberg stated, unless there is a fundamental
change in the brain, religion and spirituality
will be here for a very long time. The brain
is predisposed to having those experiences and
that is why so many people believe in God.

Now, let's take a look at how we can live in
a grand field of potentials, which may look

Deborah Baker-Receniello, PhD, CLSC

chaotic and still maintain our dreams and manifestations. Like a great master once said, Be in the world, yet not of the world.

134

Chapter 11

Field Theory: Living within the Chaotic

Man is a magnet, and every line
And dot and detail of his
Experience come by his own attraction.
The Life Power and How to Use it, by
Elizabeth Towne

Field theory can open us to thinking of the universe that resembles an ocean, filled with interrelating influences, waves and invisible structures that connect. There is a potential for action anywhere or any when two or more fields meet. Sounds familiar, whenever two or more are gathered, great things occur.

Through journeying through this book you see the value of knowing a combination of culture, values, vision, ethics, and attitudes to describe a quality of life that we can observe in our experience. Yet, it is elusive to pin down the specifics. You can see the human organism—a person (material). Yet you do not see the elusive specifics that make that person what they are—fluctuating fields (non-material).

Here, matter and energy, mind and spirit, are not really different things, only aspects of an expanded reality or two sides of the same coin.

Field theory can help us to understand ourselves more. A vision of health, clarity about purpose, and direction—all good candidates for field theory. Linearly, you can think of your goal as thinking into the future, creating a destination. The more clearer the vision or goal, the more force the future would exert on the present, pulling you into that desired future state. What if it was seen in field theory, which is non-linear?

If the goal is desired, what can you do differently to create that new vision? First you would want it to be strong enough to permeate through the entire body then radiate outwardly to every part of our lives so that everyone that bumped into it would be influenced by it. Their behavior could be shaped as a result of a field meeting another field. Their energy would link with the field's form to create behavior congruent with the vision or goal. Remember, fields can influence behavior and can cohere and organize separate events. In most reality, it is the field that controls, not the unconscious human.

You can now see yourself as broadcaster, tall radio beacons of information, pulsing out messages everywhere. If all of you are talking, clarifying, discussing, modeling and filling all of space with messages you care about, what would happen? When this is done, fields develop and their wondrous capacity to bring energy into form. There are no unimportant players.

In the natural world, fields may continue to propagate. Once created, they will sustain themselves. It is necessary therefore, to be conscious of the field creation and its impact. If a vision (field) were coherent and sincere, it would be welcomed back. It is also important to remember that space is full of waves. It should be filled with coherent messages, if you say one thing but do another, then you create dissonance in the very space of the field, then the behavior will mirror those contradictions—jumble the behaviors in different directions. You lose when you no longer walk our talk. You lose the partnership of a field-rich space that can help bring form and order to yourself. That's important to remember when surrounding yourself with those that support your endeavors, the dream makers. This is true in your personal life, your business, and your relationships.

Rupert Sheldrake, a British plant physiologist, calls this "formative causation." In his book, *A New Science of Life*, he proposes that systems are regulated not only by the laws known to physical science but also by invisible organizing field, what he calls "morphogenetic fields" (from the Greek morphe, "form" and genesis "coming into being").

If you apply Sheldrakes's theory to the development of higher consciousness, you might predict that the more individuals begin to raise their own levels of consciousness, the stronger the morphogenetic field for high states would become and easier it would be for other to move in that direction. Perhaps given the right triggers, you have the ability to produce such experiences for yourself.

Then what if, you adjust your eyes magically to the invisible world? There you can find multiple structures—potentially—can you stop doubting? Once you felt secure in the things that were visible, now you can feel secure in those things invisible; the void, Mind of God, Quantum foam. Is it time to embrace the invisible? A place where the substance of everything is something you cannot see? You don't see gravity, yet it works. You don't see love, yet it works. All it takes is the faith of the mustard seed—space awaits us filled with possibilities.

Creative individuals like artists, composers and writers have always appreciated the need for a measure of dissonance and irregularity within rule and order. The original stories of other cultures, particularly those in the East, suggest that rather than chaos emerging from the breakdown of order, it is chaos that is the generative source of the universe. Perhaps we can interchange chaos with potentiality.

Chaos is then a part of greater nonlinear dynamic that goes beyond the simple regular ideas of Newtonian physics. Nonlinear dynamics deals with abrupt and catastrophic changes, random motions, infinite sensitivity and crossroads in the evolution of a system (bifurcation points).

James Gleick, author of "Chaos: Making a new Science" says that chaos describes the apparent disorganization of open systems as though they were attempting to jiggle themselves into higher order. Does this sound like potentials turning into probabilities and then into reality?

The greater the turbulence and the more complex the solution result in the greater jump to a higher order. Sounds like a quantum pop. You can also apply Planck's time theory. Time is only a point of now with infinitely possibility, non-linear, and omnidirectional.

At the onset of chaos, as a time dimension and the ridge of chaos its pattern sets the stage for the classical chaos attractor. The 'edge' infers abrupt change.

The opportunity for rapid change to the dynamic state lies beyond the ridge of chaos, not at the abrupt chasm of turmoil, but a downward slop toward randomness. This is a vulnerable time when energy from other sources can reflect the system so that it fluctuates back and forth on the ridge, becoming neither strictly ordered, nor random. When the chaotic attractor (the observer) appears, there is an increasing likelihood of resonating and transacting with other vibrations. Newtonian Physics describes this as a 'phase shift', where some information drops out or changes—as when a solid changes from a solid to a gas. Perhaps, quantum physics would say the observer influence.

There are times at the 'ridge state' when the system is in exquisite control, balanced between order and disorder. You experience this in our consciousness when you subtly shift between material, and higher or spiritual awareness, or when you are mediating and arrive at a sudden illumination or profound sense of knowing—the Ah Ha experience!

Within the human field, it is exciting to realize that you could creatively use the flexibility of the 'ridge of chaos' to change behavior and thoughts to our advantage. There is growing evidence that in expanded consciousness, you have access to the primary reality of frequencies. Living is a transaction, an interaction with other force fields, with an element of choice. This is a domain beyond time, space and mass where only vibrations exist. Consciousness may insert information into its environment as well as extract information from it.

Every living moment is generated out of an inherently nonlinear process. The mind has the capacity for endless creativity and its functions are infinitely subtle. Yet, the mind is not limited by any context or plan and can always transcend the limits in which it is placed. It can play for play's sake; it can make a joke. It can question the context in which it finds itself and transcend its own rules; evolve.

Edward Lorenz, in his talk entitled, Predictabilty: Does the Flap of a Butterfly's Wings in Brazil set of a Tornado in Texas?", gives a great example of how a small system as a butterfly being responsible for creating such a large and distant system as a tornado in Texas to illustrates the essential idea of chaos theory.

In your lives today a number of major crises and problems appear so serious, situations whose balance is so critical, that they cry out for action. Yet, action that is not intelligently guided can lead to even worse problems, as you all know, for health, happiness, relationships, and organizations. Rushing in to fix what appears to be wrong may not be the best solution. The paradox to take action or paralysis is a frustrating one.

In a state of watchful or focused attention, as the observer, you can learn to reach out and little by little make a series of exploratory actions. When you have a fairly good idea of the extent of your actions, then the physical intervention is advisable. In this state of watchful suspension or focused attention, there is a heightened awareness and a deeper understanding of the overall situation. Creative suspension or attention allows us to get in touch with our whole pattern of reactions, rigidities, limited structures and conditioning, and the rigidities within any relationship, illness, or organization.

The idea is to observe the whole nature of intention, action and conditioning. When watchful and attentive, you are alert and it becomes possible to perceive how this intention unfolds and acts through the mind and body. In the gap of the paradox, there is a way of transcending the dilemma by allowing an infinitesimal gap in which the whole intention to act or suppress, is allowed to expand and work its way through.

Being watchful and attentive allows you to observe the way certain words evoke physical reaction within your body and how this physical reaction can, in turn, trigger other thoughts and words or modify their meanings. *This allows the gap between intention and action to lie beyond time and enables the mind to touch a creative perception and enter a new order*. This suggests that your capacity for creating new and highly subtle responses may be far greater than we realize. When you free yourself of fixed patterns and blocks, you will tap into an unlimited source of creativity.

In the process of writing this book and forming a new organization, I have learned about ownership and the power of intention. Ownership constricts, even the most expansive mind. We cannot own the void, Mind of God, or the quantum. What really makes you think we can truly own anything? You can have stewardship and use, but not really own. With this attitude you are free again.

You can establish ourselves consciously on a frontier that has been hidden, yet an unstoppable part of us, and life itself. Life is not our personal backdrop that has to conform to us -it is a force to inspire, mirror, and play with us. When you become aware of the invisibility of creation and through co-creation we can allow each pattern or blueprint speak to us in its own language, acts and love. You can pay real attention to the world; it is alive. You can communicate with and let it communicate with us and engage life.

My emotional investment desires to have an organization that works for me and for those involved with me. Stewardship inspires and creates personal links to the organization, the charged, emotion-driven feeling of inspiration. People support what they love and create. The quantum universe supports this concept even more strongly than I imagined and it also explains how it creates real and tangible sources of energy. It is important to let go of ownership and allow the creation process to those who will be charged with its implementation.

Being involved in the design process, all of us experience the plan as a living, breathing thing. Building a sense of play with all the different possibilities through our own personal process of observation.

This watchful state is not to 'do nothing' or to block external activity, but allows me to be alert with myself, and those I work with. It's my job to hold the intent of my desires and allow that to unfold and enfold into fruition. Not seeking to control, which sets me outside and separate from my desire, but to have the barriers between inner and outer dissolve and let the fixed responses give way to fluid actions that form new active perception. This also allows for the dream or

143

intent to carry through and not necessarily be in a linear fashion. It has room to evolved and become greater in an infinite way.

We marvel at the ease of meetings, the creativity, inspiration and the formation. Nothing is independent to the relationship of our world. The ability to evoke it and participate in all its many interactions, this is a world of process, not things. When I think of all those wave functions filling space, rich in potentials, I wonder why limit ourselves so quickly to one idea or one perception. Why stay locked in a belief that there is one right way to do something, when the universe welcomes diversity and thrives on multiplicity of meanings? What a wonderful world it can be, when we look at the events and interactions rather than to things and thus become. My dream is to continue the dance and vary the tempo—so that which supports the process develops and forms relationships to support the enfoldment.

Why not? To use the power of God, Nature, quantum and the Divine ability of thought for experience to become the explorer in the vast ocean of potentially. You could then change roles or models of reality from old paradigms to new realities, evolved realities. Why not use the science as a tool to understand reality and participate in a life well lived and joyfully to evolve ideas.

The void, Mind of God, or quantum is the implicate order of which all potential exists. Are we able to explicate matter by focused intentional will, imagination and dreams to create the order of an implicate mind?

To paraphrase from Nelson Mandela's inaugural address of 1994:

Our fear is not that we are inadequate. Our deepest fear is power, beyond measure. We ask who am I to be brilliant, vibrant, gorgeous, talented, sure-footed, and fabulous. Actually, we should ask, why not?

There is nothing enlightening about playing small, to hide or diminish your being-ness so others around you do not feel insecure. This does not serve the world. You have a cosmic mandate, you are on a journey to personal exploration and expansion—make known the unknown—When you do, through your own actions, presence or being-ness; you liberate others to do the same. You are born to manifest the glory of God within all of us.

Your brain is a micro-bio-computer and each is the programmer. You, unconscious beings, can be limited by your past experience, education, religion, culture or political beliefs or You, conscious beings, can be as unlimited as you venture to become. It's your choice!

When you realize your focused thoughts affect life—that's when you take responsibility of timing or focusing your thoughts. It takes constant vigil to be the guardian at the gate, the observer, and only allow productive or wise thoughts to emanate. If your thoughts run wild, they'll destroy you. Your words are your manifestations.

Deborah Baker-Receniello, PhD, CLSC

It is you who chooses to see, interpret, and feel—anything. In a moment, your life can change.

Perhaps making a list of what you want in life can help keep you focused. Ask yourself:

What do I want in Life?
What haven't I experienced?
How do I use more than the 10% of my brain?
What is my potential?
I want to live longer, so I can know!
If I can hold that thought long enough, could I, as observer apply that law and collapse the wave function into a new reality?
Is joy being the lord of the physical, not it's slave?
Can I change my timeline, as I know it in this moment?

Sir Francis Bacon once said, the right to investigate is the credo of free men—this opportunity to try, this privilege to err, this courage to experiment anew.

Perhaps you have to blow the circuits of everyday ideology or superstructure of belief held. You are a consciousness on a journey to personal exploration and expansion and perhaps a way to examine various aspects of who you are.

Whether you speak of Physiology, Biology, Psychology, Physics, Mathematics, Religion, or Philosophy – you use a language to describe something that may be unfamiliar in your lives. Matter and energy, mind and spirit, are not really different things, only aspects of an expanded reality. Isn't it time to take

146

charge, have courage to make it familiar, and use it to define your selves differently?

You are not human beings who are having spiritual experiences. You are really spiritual beings who are having a human experience. Until now, you have played the game well. Now, with additional knowledge, in your own time, all the borders that confine your reality will begin to fade.

Your life, up to now, could have been a train wreck. Perhaps you settled, messed up, got busy surviving, got busy playing roles of other's expectancies, or just got too busy. Most people get up in the morning and instead of working on your mind and your heart for even five minutes, you will obsess around for one to two hours, focusing totally on your appearance instead of your substance. Stop and think how much of your life's energy is caught up in the superficial rather than what you know in your heart really matters. You know that 'the stuff of you' really matters and what's in your heart really matters.

Here's the challenge. In order for you ever to effectively change, map out how to get to where you want to go, you have to know exactly where you are starting. Where you are now, everything you are, everything you do, begins and is based on what is your personal truth. Everything that you believe about yourself is absolutely true.

The magnitude of the glorious journey ahead is ready to be defined by you. It's work and you have to be committed, or dare I say, aware.

Let's look at the process.

PART II

Getting what you Desire: The Process

"You cannot teach a man anything; you Can only help him to find it within Himself..." Galileo

"Americans are less complacent that others When told our dreams will not come true. We are not Patient in the face of rejected dreams because we have Always been told we have a right to have them. We Are literally born into the promise and that America Is the land where dreams come true..."
                    Marianne Williamson

Just do it!

This part of the book is a work in progress, a combination of self-work and workshops over the years. Each time I do this, it seems to expand and include more pieces of the puzzle or something changes a bit to become even more powerful. If you uncover a more empowering process or addition to this, please, by all means share it with me so that I can share it with others. By sharing what you have learned you will be expanding and reinforcing your own consciousness and you will be expanding the consciousness of others in the world at large.

For more information, a private coaching consultation, or to inquire into hosting or attending a workshop on the manifestation process or individual area of interest, or having Dr. Baker Receniello speak, please email:

email: dbrcoaching@comcast.net
www.dbrlifecoach.com

It matters not the language of quantum physics, Physiology, Biology, Psychology, Mathematics, Religion, or Philosophy - you can use a language to describe something that may be unfamiliar in your lives. Matter and energy, mind and spirit, are not really different things, only aspects of an expanded reality. Isn't it time to take charge, have courage to make it familiar, and use it to define your selves differently?

Here is a list of **Qualities of a Creator or Dream Maker:**

1. Every Dream Maker **understands there is a web of energy:**

   This web permeates everything and it is intelligent. It responds to human emotion, thoughts, and creates vibrations that have the ability to heal the cells of our body or any circumstance. Some call it the Mind of God, others Quantum Physics, or the Void.

2. Every Dream Maker has a **VISION:**

   They can tell you in great detail what they wanted and where they were going. They could see, smell, taste, feel and sense what success is when they get it. They see the future.

3. Every Dream Maker knows to **use positive, loving statements** to create. To create the experience of the dream itself and not the experience of hope, wish, want, need or try.

e.g. Hoped a situation would get better
Wished you were healthy
Wanted to be happier
Needed more money
Tried to do something or fix something

These create just an experience of hoping, wishing, wanting, needing or trying and not the actual dream. Ever need more money and have it disappear. It is interpreted, as your dream is to need more not have it.

Ever want a new car. Then your existing car needs repair. The experience of wanting a car is created instead of the actual car.

Using any of these scenarios, you have created an experience of 'want' and found your present situation either continuing unchanged or worsening, because you actually created it into your own reality.

4. Every Dream Maker has **clarity and chooses the results**.

Ever created a job to have money, so you can buy something or spend the money on something that made your happy. It isn't until the last 'create happiness' that the universe became aware that the experience you desired was happiness in the first place. If so, then working for the money would not have been necessary in order to achieve happiness. This is like sneaking in the back door.

5. Every Dream Maker has **PASSION**:

They are excited, can't wait to get up in the morning. Their vision holds deep meaning. Passion is love. Love permeates all life.

6. Dream Makers are aware of the timeframe, **Now, Present moment**.

Their past doesn't exist n emotion—only the wisdom gained from the experience. The never use phrases such as:

Going to
Will be
Eventually
Some day
In the near future
Soon
Later
When it's supposed to be
IF it's meant to be

Create an open-ended timeframe. If you say, "I am going to start a new successful venture", then the success of that experience may never happen because of going to.

A better way to state this is: My new venture reached $1, 000,000 sales in December, 2003. I have 15+ staff members, etc.

7. Dream makers **know with certitude**.

If you do not believe something, it's because you have not had the experience yet to know it is true. Get the education of what the dream is about, visualize or imagine it over and over. When you accept the dream it becomes the experience. When dreaming, it is imperative to know that it is already done.

8. Every Dream Maker has a **STRATEGY**:

They have a plan. Every Dream Maker has **PRIORITIES**. They know when to say "no" and when to say, "yes" in order to stay on the path to their goals. They know the responsibility of each act and takes responsibility for themselves.

9. Every Dream Maker has **ENERGY**.

They take care of themselves both physically and emotionally. They have a healthy lifestyle and do not stay in relationships that are draining.

10. Every Dream Maker has a nucleus of **PEOPLE** around them who are excited for them, support them and are invested in them (Dream Makers, not Dream Breakers).

Creating Vision

"For all those years you've protected the seed
It's time to become the beautiful flower.
Stephen C. Paul

Your vision of what you desire is your blueprint of your actions. Define the focus of your desire. This would mean writing down the highest thoughts you can think about your desire. It would incorporate your highest values or what you care about. Vision sets the state for Clarity, Focus and Action and in alignment provides coherence. It is a statement of what you are in relationship with the desire. Your vision will open a new level of thinking and feeling and more creativity. When this vision is accomplished, it provides complete fulfillment.

I realized my calling is to Coach, write, speak, and conduct workshops. Just get that word out there.

Today, I hold a vision of what I chose. I see prosperity, clients, joyous experiences, amazing miracles, and surrounded by loved ones. Now the doors are flying open. Life is magical!

I now create clients, loving relationship with the man who more than meets my ideal qualities, my son is doing well, and am creating brilliant, creative work. I am writing more than ever and even started to illustrate the books. I didn't know I could paint. I facilitate workshops all over the U.S. and expand where needed.

Make the decision to create your life full of joy, excitement, abundance, happiness, love, health, prosperity and success! Let go of the stories from the past that have held you back and live consciously to see the miracles unfold. Love yourself, and trust the Universe to make your dreams your reality.

Manifesting

Whether you know it or not, whether you like it or not, you are continuously manifesting all aspects of our lives through your thoughts and our feelings. Whatever you give great emotional feeling to begin to be created and the Mind of God, Mind Field or the Void is all too happy to give it to you and supports your intentional or unconscious beliefs.

Manifesting, is defined by Webster as:
"The act or process of instance of manifesting. Manifest easily understood by the mind; readily perceived by the senses; a future event accepted as inevitable." The last one is the one I love most. You have the power to put forth into your life whatever you choose with purpose. To manifest is to bring into materialism. Materialism to make material; that which is perceived by the senses, understood by the mind and a future experience accepted as inevitable.

If we are conscious about our choices through the power that is given to us, we can manifest the life of our dreams. We need to simply place an order with clarity, filled with love and gratitude, and know it is delivered with certitude. Now we have the knowledge of the sciences and the knowledge of manifestation.

As my great teacher use to say, now, let's get to work!

List your top TEN Current Dreams

1.

2.

3.

4.

5.

6.

7.

8.

9.

10.

I. For the purpose of this exercise: Prioritize these Dreams and pick the # 1 Dream

1

2

3

4

5

6

7

8

9

10

1. Dream

II. Take # 1 Dream and answer these questions:

1. What do you desire:

2. Use   Positive   terms
    specific,   sensory-based
    description of outcome.

3. What will you and others
    see, hear, feel, etc?

4. What will my #1 Dream look
    like when I manifest it?
    How will I feel?

5. It is appropriate size to manage or do I have to put it onto manageable chunks?

6. How will my life change?

7. What is the prize? What will having this dream do for you?

8. What prevents you from having this dream now?

9. What additional resources do you need to get your outcome? Check for negative self-talk, educating yourself, beliefs, distortions, or generalizations. What are you willing to change or do to manifest this dream?

10. What resources do you already have that will contribute to getting to dream?

III. **Modifying the Dream:**

1. Follow steps 1-7 to redefine your dream: Write a scene about the # 1 Dream.

IV. **Look at the scene you have just written.**

1. To get to the #1 Dream Mind, you must FIND and ELIMINATE your limited beliefs. Remember how the brain works! Go through your scene and circle any word that triggers a thought or

belief that feels negative, gnaws at you or strikes a cord.

2. Take each belief and elaborate as much as possible for the purpose or greater clarity about where you are with this belief and what you need to do to change it, to improve yourself or expand your dream consciousness

3. Add or change any belief that needs to be addressed that is not aligned with your Dream.

V. Eliminate negative beliefs

a. You could interview several people about the belief and ask, "is it true?"

b. Contemplate where and when you made the judgment or belief, ask yourself. Is it still true today?

c. Use Muscle Testing to reveal beliefs. (See appendix 7)

d. Ask, "Am I willing to eliminate this negative belief and choose another experience?"

e. Ask, "Am I willing to choose a new experience and am I worthy to deserve what I want?"

If you are willing to accept the change, then there are several techniques to eliminate these negative beliefs.

Here's one that I especially like.

You write a letter to yourself, higher power or God.

In it you write the date, what you cease to believe in, state that you are willing and ready to accept your unlimited potential and to accept that you deserve what you want. Then, state that this day, you renounce your human-hood or your past experiences and claim your Divine inheritance. This day you acknowledge the Mind of God, Void or Quantum, etc. as your platform, your supply and support, lay out the new experience as you desire it. Sign it!

This really works. If you don't feel confident to do this, then write the letter to the effectiveness of the process. It still works.

Here's an example of one that I wrote:

On this ___ day of ____, 2003, I cease believing in visible money as my supply and my support and I view the world of effect as it is...simply an out picturing of my former beliefs. I believed in the power of money, therefore I surrendered my God-given power and authority to a limited dream. I believed in lack, and created a separation my consciousness from the source of supply. I believed in the created collective consciousness of error thoughts and became limited.

NO MORE!

This day I renounce (or I completely release) the old beliefs and all behaviors, thoughts, people, places, events that contributed to this limitation.

This day I accept my unlimited potential and accept I deserve my dream of fabulous wealth.

This day, I acknowledge God and only God as my substance, my supply and my support.
Signed this _____ day of _____

So Be It!

Use the technique of Scripting or Making a mental movie.

SCRIPTING

Allow yourself to be in a place with no interruptions. Make sure you know what it is you want to change or do differently.

Begin by relaxing the body. Breathing deeply, relaxing each muscle group from your head to your toes.

Recall a positive experience or an optimal moment. Immerse yourself in all the senses of this experience. Identify the state.

When you are ready bring the image of what you want to re-script upon the screen of your mind or imagine being at the movies and watching the image or scene on the screen. Allow it to play to the point you want to change it.

Now, stop the movie. Reverse the film. Replay what you want to change, the way you want to change it. Change the words, feelings, environment, scents, etc. Remember to breathe deeply and allow the body to stay relaxes. Here is your ideal performance. Enjoy it.

Remember the positive experience or optimal moment you identified earlier. Access it now. Relive it, now.

Bridge this feeling with the new performance you just created.

It is done.

Allow yourself to revel in this new experience. When you are ready, slowly allow the curtains to close. Bring your consciousness awareness back to where you are

VI. Create a new and improved Dream—Get Dream Minded!

If you want to be successful and prosperous then you must not contemplate any thoughts of failure, unworthy, should haves, could haves or poverty. You can no longer think in past terms or habits that perpetuate anything but your new dream. After you cease and desist all limiting beliefs, now you need to expand your dream consciousness.

Now it's time to model enlightened (en light of) beings.

MODELING

As *Webster* defines it, Modeling means: to design a set of plans for something; a miniature representation of something or a pattern of something to be made; an example for imitation or emulation, a person or thing that serves as a pattern; an organism whose appearance mimics or imitates; a description or analogy used to help visualize something that cannot be directly observed; a system of postulates, data, and inferences presented as a mathematical description of an entity or state of affairs; to plan, pattern, shape an ideal.

The use of modeling is not a new concept to most of us. Perhaps modeling used to change a behavior, change an attitude; project into a new environment can be used more efficiently and successfully for each of us. Athletic trainers have been using this technique for years to improve performance. Quantum physics verifies all the new discoveries in the use of imaging as a precursor to the creation of conscious reality.

In your mind you can practice something perfectly and create a neural network of perfect execution. The practice of experiencing in the now moment whatever you desire to be, is the most powerful technique you can use to become anything you desire.

A. PLAN
   1. Design a set of plans: What is it you would like to do or change?
   1. Make a miniature representation of something or pattern: Here is a place for lots of creative ventures. Cut out a picture; draw a symbol, use imagination and visualization. (You can Mind Map, create a collage, create a dream book)

B. EDUCATE YOURSELF

   An example for imitation or emulation, a person or thing that serves as a pattern: It's like a dress rehearsal, act like it until it is so. If you admire certain traits of a person, model them. Read about their life, their accomplishments, their practices, their strengths and desires.

Collect data. Educate yourself, if you do not know how to do something. Read or speak with people who are financial genius or have that special skill you desire. Remember your mind will only give you what it knows. Listen to a tape of them speaking. Watch them in a movie or documentary or their daily life. Feed your mind to help amp up your energy and intent.

VII. Use Your Imagination

The key to understanding how creative visualization or imagination works is that your subconscious mind does not know what is real or what is fiction. It lives in a no time state. It can create a scene to use as a memory for a future event to manifest.

Visualize something like an apple. You can describe it from your memory of an apple; you may see it in the mind's eye. Imagination is taking something you know and embellishing it. Like the apple, turn its color blue. Move inside it, what's the texture, etc.

Plan, pattern, and shape an ideal: Explore the ideal you desire, focus on it, let in roll around in your mind, educate yourself with new knowledge, how would you be, *free your mind to imagine!*

Think of it like going to a Cosmic Restaurant somewhere in the universe.

169

When you enter the restaurant and the waiter appears, you don't want to tell the waiter that you want "food." You need to be more definite than that. Tell him what you want, how you want it and when. We don't say, "salad". We usually would say, green garden salad, topped with chicken, dressing on the side, no bread and water plain, no ice.

Here's an example that went wrong.

I just had a new house built in a lovely neighborhood, near New Orleans. I decided I want a new, shinny red Mercedes, 350SL convertible. I used focused imagery. I saw the car in the driveway. I did this religiously for months. I remember walking outside and I could feel the energy building in the driveway. But, still no car.

I got a call asking me to go to Santa Fe, New Mexico to head up a research project with a private corporation. I was really excited about that and told them, yes.

Now I have to do something with my new home. I leased it. The gentleman who leased the home owned, you guessed it—A Mercedes, 350SL convertible, RED. Thus, the car IS in the drivew

Always put yourself into the dream! Drive the car, feel the wind in your hair, smell the interior leather, listen to the stereo or CD, show your friends. Travel somewhere.
Love the car and be grateful for the experience of having it.

Now, you do it the right way with passion!

VIII. Make a Dream Book or Treasure Map

Sages say, "A picture is worth a thousand words." This is true because images are the way the subconscious mind processes information. A word or verbal phrase translates into images in the inner mind.

Cut out and collect pictures from magazines that represent what you want. The action of finding the pictures, cutting them out, then paste them onto paper helps to convince the subconscious that you really do want this goal. The pictures may simply evoke the feeling of the desired result, such as a sunset for peace, or a lit candle for enlightenment, or specific pictures of a cruise, car, income or job. The idea is to find pictures that speak to you. For a job, you might find pictures of someone doing that specific job, or a picture that symbolizes it to you.

Underneath the pictures, you write an affirmation that directs the mind. The affirmation can be "I know that my Higher Mind wants this for me, and my creative mind finds the best way for it to manifest" or "I now have a lavish income of X coming to me easily and freely." Any statement that clarifies your goal and supports the belief that Spirit is manifesting it now will work. This helps keep you aware that the Universe wants this for you as much as you want it for yourself.

There are different ways to use the basic technique. For a single goal, such as a job, relationship, travel, or new house or car, you can get a page of colored construction paper or large poster and paste the pictures on it. Use a color that connects with you and your goal. Such as green or gold for prosperity, blue or green for relationships or relaxation, red or orange for a new position or some change in your life, purple or lavender for spiritual growth. I had a friend who created a treasure map and placed it on the inside of the door to her closet, where she saw it every day. You can also use a corkboard or Styrofoam to pin the pictures and affirmations to, and change them as you choose.

For several different goals, you can get a poster and divide it into the areas of your goals. You could segment it into four parts, such as: work, play, relationships, and health. Then paste the pictures and write the affirmations as you would with a single sheet in each area. At the center, you could have a picture and affirmation that recognizes that the Universe is the Source of your good.

You can use a notebook for your treasure map. Keep it in a drawer of your desk to look at several times a day. You can take a folder with fasteners, like you used in school, and put pictures and affirmations on sheets of paper. Again, each goal should have its own separate sheet of paper.

With a treasure map, you need to have it where you can look at it several times a day, but where no one else can see it, such as a closet or drawer. This keeps it private, between you and your Higher Self. If you have someone who will be completely supportive of your goal, you can share. Look at your map several times a day and each time give thanks that the Universe and your creative mind has already given you what the pictures represent. By giving your mind a picture of your desire, keeping your attention focused on it, the Universe will find the perfect way to transport you to your destination.

Make a symbol or drawing of the desire or new plan

This is similar to the Dream Book or Treasure Map. This one can be portable.

Use 4" x 6" index cards, crayons, pens, paint, glitter, etc.

Create a symbol of what the manifested dream or goal is

Be sure to concentrate on the manifestation as if you already have it, love it and are doing it.

Keep the card handy to look at often or place it where you can see it often. This acts as a trigger to the subconscious mind of what you want and keeps you on track.

IX. Make a sacred place

Somewhere make a place that is special to you. Use what makes you feel energized, peaceful and creative (candles, incense, waterfall, music, stones, miniatures, pictures, outdoors).

This is where you will begin your manifestation process. You will want it away from interruptions.

X. Focused Intentional Will

Focused intent is an expression that refers to applied thought directed at expressing your values and vision in your everyday life. The human mind has great creative potential. There is a way to begin to access more of your creative potential, which is amazingly simply and effective for many people. Be Open to the possibility of the 'Genie" within you.

INTENT: Intent means an established plan so that personal energy will be activated and take a general direction. We fix our mind on thoughts that are material or immaterial. Intent is a purpose that implies an end result. Your intent must be strong, clear and captured.

Remember intent is personal to you. It must be appropriate to you, dedicated and serious with a singleness of purpose and that intent must be primary. All the thoughts and beliefs you have had in the past about the problem are secondary to this process and eventually become eliminated. This is the vital part for success. Your powerful new intent directs new emotion/energy to eliminate any prior programmed information or imprinted of what caused the problem. Always remember, your past is not your future, UNLESS you live there.

FOCUS: This is the change. To imprint new information upon the dendrites of the brain you must be able to focus actively to direct your energies toward the outcome. You used your sensory input, visual, emotional, tactile, color or sound. Focus is the tool you use to *amplify* your intent.

Make a Focused Intent Dream. Start with one dream, when you are successful, then make the dream list or focused intent list containing more than one dream.

1. Set aside a few moments at the beginning of each day to sit quietly and write on a blank piece of paper what you would like to see in your life or business in the near future. Use your dream book, treasure map or symbol cards.

2. Go to your sacred place.

   a. Make sure others know you will be there for a while. Find a comfortable place.
   b. Close your eyes after looking at your dreams/desires.
   c. Take a few deep breaths. Relax the body and calm your mind. This is the place where you become aware of the Mind of God, Mind Field or Matrix of all there is. Just breathe in this field. This allows you to feel love and peace.
   d. Visualize or imagine your goals, dreams, and desires. You can see the

    picture and say the affirmations to yourself.

    e. Love what you see

    f. Surrender to the dream

    g. Express gratitude

    h. Open your eyes. Now take action in your world

3. After a few days, make a note of any reoccurring theme(s). Make note of these.

4. Take your reoccurring theme(s) and make a list

5. Create a picture or drawing to correspond to your new list. Take out crayon, paper, index cards, etc. Be like a child and create your symbol or drawing to incorporate everything that you know.

6. Choose a time each day when you will spend 15 minutes or more, reviewing the list and visualizing the pictures or drawings.

7. Be consistent every day for at least three weeks, without an attachment to the outcome.

8. After this time, review your thoughts about your list.
Have they changed anyway?
Have you become more focused in your daily actions?
Have you made different choices about your time and list?
Have you added new items or changed the language to better express your intent?
How many items have you accomplished?

9. Over the next few months, continue to develop and review your list DAILY. You'll be pleasantly surprised at the ease of your outcome.

10. Let me know of your results

11. You are more powerful; even beyond your imagination, aren't you?

XI. Meditation

The basic idea generally associated with why people meditate is that during our day we are constantly bombarded with sensory input and our minds run away, usually with the drama of life or ME. We read the newspaper, listen to the news on TV or radio, engage in conversation, solve problems, etc. This creates a lot of mental thought activity that we are constantly engaged in. Meditation allows us an opportunity to settle down and often results in the mind becoming more peaceful, calm and focused. In essence, it's rejuvenation.

It usually involves stilling the chattering mind and focus on a specific object, thought, or sound, or enter the complete stillness of the Void; all are examples of meditation. Over time the random thoughts begin to diminish. Your attachment to these thoughts and identification will progressively become lessened. There are many varied methods, you can seek out which works best for you.

Meditation allows your brain to function at an alpha brainwave frequency and with added practice to eventually enter a waking theta frequency. In these states you will find a space of open and creative mind. Meditation is a great way to relax, let go, increase awareness, mental focus and clarity, and connect with something much grander.

Creative mind is always present in the space between the altered ego and a spontaneous self-aware intuitive moment. It can be learned.

XII. Guided Imagery

Using all the senses, not just visual, some background music, or nature sounds, a narrator leads the way through relaxation techniques into an inner journey. Along the way, affirmations may be used.

Guided imagery recordings or live sessions with a coach provide a general guide to pull your mind and body away from the chatter and stimuli of everyday life. The images and words are only a springboard for your own unique inner journey. Guided imagery is a powerful, yet simple way of creating peacefulness in the body, mind, emotions and allows you to bring in what is desired.

Anyone can benefit from this technique; people with illnesses, athletes, artists, hard working fold, children and adults.

Guided Imagery can help you change the body chemistry, digest emotions, allow the mind to access intelligence and set the spirit free. It can release performance anxiety, worries, hurts or distresses. It can assist in any learning or healing program.

There are many guided imagery and subliminal tapes on the market. Do your research.

XIII. Forgiveness and Gratitude

If you haven't already addressed Forgiveness and Gratitude in releasing old limited beliefs, let's take a look at it now. It's important to become aware of how the smallest resentment can wreak havoc on our dreams.

Any time we entertain the emotion of anger, bitterness, condemnation and resentment, we are sowing the seeds of doubt and limitations. Remember how energy seeks its level. Even if we have the loftiest dream and have these negative emotions, we are brought down to its level of manifestation.

These negative emotions, like weeds, can create havoc and strangle our most beautiful dream garden. We have to mind our gardens, tending our dreams with the fertilizer of love, acceptance and unlimited adventures. When you remember the past, remember selectively the love, beauty or strength that was learned from an event instead of holding on to resentment, loss or fear. Remember the science!

We all must make that commitment to weed ourselves of all that emotionally drains us, takes our power and leaves us weakened. There is a lot of freedom in letting go, acceptance and understanding. An older teacher has always reminded me, "They didn't know any better, or they would have done better".

Remember that everything in life seems to be plastic. You can mold it to fit what you want and where you want to go. You can always play with new possibilities.

Make the commitment to forgive. A simple statement is very powerful. Remember how the brain works!

I completely and totally forgive _____. I send forth love and blessings to you and yours.

I release anything and everything that no longer serves my greater good.

I forgive myself.

Let's look at what GRATITUDE can do!

1. Gratitude is the easiest way to change REALITY. Remember what physics and brain function taught us. Reality is how we perceive the situation, not what's happening. We, at any given time, have the opportunity to follow through in a situation or to change what's happening before us.

   Anytime we perceive a potential threat, fear, or less than best situation, we can always give thanks for the perfect outcome. I lost my balance and came crashing down on my knee first, then hip and then elbow. I was scattered in my thinking. I remembered I can accept the consequences I create. My husband helped me stand. I told him I was okay. Then fear crept in with the pain. I decided to see the doctor right away to confirm I was okay. He took an x-ray. He was amazed that I had not fractured or broken the kneecap and dislocated my hip. He commented that a normal person of my age would have. He also was amazed at the amount of cushion in my knee joint. He said, "Whatever you are doing, keep it up."

2. Gratitude creates miracles in ways you can't possibly imagine. Early on, I attended a seminar on writing. I did not have any business cards. I realized that I was feeling a little insecure about my writing, when approaching a publisher. Once I cleared my insecurity and had a clear intent of being in service, I realized I was in the right place. I was grateful to do what I love. I appreciate people who inspire me. I see examples around me daily of successful people. Now the world comes to me. Hence, the success of my books, my coaching practice and workshops.

3. Gratitude heals difficult situations. My son was having a difficult time with his hormonal teenage years. Every thing that didn't work would set him off. I suggested he look at his anger and discover what was at the bottom. One technique used was to create what goes

right! Being thankful for what was right in his life.

4. Appreciate your moments. Become grateful for life coursing through your veins. Become grateful for the food you eat, how it gives you energy and how the body eliminates what it doesn't need. Be grateful for the people in your life, they are a mirror.

5. Create a journal of gratitude and record something each day.

6. Remember that your inner state of being attracts and creates your outer results—and what to do about it so you can have, do or be whatever your heart desires.

7. Gratitude sets you up with love. Remember what love has to do with manifesting!

XIV. Create a room for healing

Close your eyes and take in a few deep breaths. Relax your body. See yourself inside an empty room. First appears a mentor, someone you trust with medical and healing advice. Introduce yourself and state your purpose. Inside this room, create what you will need. Create a screen for viewing the body for any diagnostics. Create a healing table. This could include sound, color, frequency, etc. You can have a computer with information at your fingertips. You can have spare parts available for transplant. Anything you want. Whenever you want to question or heal something, go to this room and meet your mentor. Then proceed as needed.

XV. Create a place for learning

Just like the healing room, only add what you may need. You can have a mentor that is a genius in a certain field for a certain project, (Great artist, musician, scientist, language expert, financial guru, etc.) A computer may be fun that is connected to the universal Internet. Any other tools you may need. Whenever you want to know something, explore or invent, use this room.

XVI. Create a spiritual haven

Do the same as above. Create the environment, tools, mentors, etc.

XVII. Create a Board Room

Visualize your boardroom with all the furniture and tools you will need. You can bring people in to discuss proposals. Let them all speak. Notice the objections. Building Solutions. Reevaluate your proposal. Now present the new proposal, practice, and see the response you desire.

Giving a speech - go to the boardroom, extend it to include the audience. Now do the speech, notice the reactions, feel confident, know your material, and get the results you intend by practice and engaging others.

XVIII. Create a Universal Bank or Account

Visualize yourself walking up the stone steps to enter the universal bank. You have an account set up already. You can make deposits, make withdrawals or negotiate financial business of any kind. Since it is a universal bank, it is limitless. Your account is always full. Whenever you need anything, just go inside and make the withdrawal or use the universal ATM.

Imagine you have a bank account and each day a certain amount is deposited. Each day you use this money. Anything left in the account disappears. The next day the original amount shows up again.

This gives you the experience of being unlimited.

XIX. Be More Creative

Now, we become aware that there is something more than just a physical body, struggling in the concept of making a living, supporting a family, providing for retirement, and ultimately, death. Now, we can be unlimited; it's the possibly of not knowing the word—*end*.

We can learn to quiet ourselves from the fury of living and doing, to the silence of being and feeling. Take a look at the quality of the human awareness around us, in our friends, acquaintances and work associates. Do we have dream-makers or dream-breakers?

Are we really being nourished, dragged down or stagnate providing nothing?

Take responsibility for our own life. We can determine the agenda to follow and choose our responses to what happens around us.

Choose more carefully where and on what you spend your free time and get more spiritual exercise. Practice regular meditation and contemplation to absorb higher vibrations and enable your mind to be elevated.

We can begin and end with Mind: Use personal vision, imagination and intuition, personal meaning to accomplish tasks in a positive and effective way. Know what drives you? Know that it may not be what you want, but how you feel about what you want that makes a difference. Continue to educate yourself.

What is it like to exercise discipline, use focused-will, plan and execute according to your priorities. "Walk your talk". Find opportunities to get in touch with your divine nature.
Participating in song and dance is a great way to increase vibrational states rather than just listening or watching.

Can we have an abundant mentality: effective communication, right thinking, spirit of cooperation and high trust level in inner self. Enjoy functioning in the midst of Chaos.

Can we become the Observer or Silent Witness and be nonjudgmental and know our own intent. We live in everyday reality of coping, solving problems, thinking, and communicating. We forget super-consciousness. Mastery is the soul's unavoidable journey; living in the world, but not of the world.

We can value and benefit from differences; know it is the whole. The most you can give to anyone is what you are—a Divine consciousness manifesting through a human body the joy of living.

Your past is not your future, UNLESS you choose to live there. Negative emotions can keep the past alive. Certain emotions that can stall or drive you are frustration and confusion. Frustration means you are on the verge of a breakthrough. Confusion can mean you are about to learn something. Expect the breakthrough and expect to learn.

Connect with Nature. Enjoy a walk, sunset, fresh scent of recently cut grass, ever-present power of the ocean, bathe in the painted hue of a mountain at sunrise.

Become **Child-like**. Enjoy, play, have fun. Stay open to opportunity and curiosity. Ask Why? Or, What if?

Become an inner, not object (outer) referred person. Object referral means that people, places, things, times and events dictates whom you are and how to respond. Happiness needs an excuse in this mode. You are seen through other's eyes, a form of conditioned response thinking or hypnosis of social conditioning. Inner Referral person feels wonderful regardless of the people, places, things, times and events. You do not need to defend yourself. Bliss is the observer and silent witness.

Become **Alive,** enjoy the miracles of life. Do not become rigidly attached to your own point of view. Look at a sunset, the life in one square foot of grass, or play in the rain. Watch nature, you may be surprised and see a gem that resembles a challenge in your own life.

Dream: Desire is pure potentiality seeking to manifest. The universal field of all possibility is waiting to interact with you. Associate yourself with Dream Makers. These are people that believe in you and give you the encouragement to take risks, persist, laugh and live your dreams.

Perhaps then, our job becomes: **Dream** it, **create** it, be **prepared to experience** it and then **own it**. Take the owning as a new architectural design or matrix and create **something better**.

If you have suggestions, email me: TakeChargeManifest@hotmail.com

XX. Attend Workshops

Take Charge: Design your life
Two-Day Workshop
Principles of the Book

Take Charge: Manifest your Dreams
Ten Weekly Sessions

One-Day Mini Workshop designed for your personal or business needs

Workshop designed for your personal or business needs Ten weeks, 2 hours each

Intro Evening
1 1/2 -2 Hours

Available for Keynotes & Conference Sessions:

Dr. Baker-Receniello's humor combined with her gentle presence and powerful message make her presentations a "must attend". If you are looking to optimize your company's employees, increase effective communication, better customer service, then make sure you hear her.

Using gentle, powerful words and examples, Deborah teaches about removing patterns and limitations that sabotage success and consciously create the life, relationships, teams and success to optimize life, now, and be living richly.

Deborah Baker-Receniello, PhD, CLSC
DBR Life & Business Coach, Inc.
PMB 209 800 Sleater Kinney SE
Lacey, WA 98501
Email: dbrcoaching@comcast.net
Webpage: www.dbrlifecoach.com

10) Life Strategies Coaching

What is Personal Coaching?

Coaching is a professional service provided clients with feedback, insights, and guidance from an outside vantage point. The business of coaching is similar to the practice of any professional.

Coaching is an on-going collaborative partnership built on taking action. In this powerful alliance, you will find yourself:

     *Doing more than you would do on your own
     *Taking yourself more seriously
     *Creating momentum and consistency
     *Taking more effective and focused actions
     *Becoming more balanced and fulfilled.

People hire a coach when they are start a new business, making a career transition, feeling dissatisfied, re-evaluating life choices, or simply looking for a personal or professional breakthrough.

What's in it for you?

With an outside perspective on your own situation, you have an advocate, a partner, and a mentor that helps you.

   **Just imagine living the life you want!
   Create the most exciting vision you can possibly create and love it!**

Have a Great Relationship

189

A Career You Love
Financial Freedom
Make better and timely decisions
Set more realistic and achievable goals
Position yourself for opportunity
Achieve balance and reduce the stress in your life
Integrate your personal and professional life
Being Enthusiastic About Life
Feeling Good About Yourself
High Profit/Productivity in your Business
Effective Communications Skills
Creativity/Genius
Healthier Lifestyle

Together, we can examine ways to balance all areas of your life, allowing you to develop mentally, emotionally, spiritually, physically, socially, and yes, professionally.

In considering a coach, you want to look for the qualities, values and integrity you would like to emulate. A good coach will also possess:

The ability to establish clarity of purpose
Keen insight into personal dynamics
Objectivity in pointing out ways to improve
Sensitivity to read between the lines
Provide complete confidentiality

Business Coaching is a confidential asset many professionals are using to build and sustain their positions as high performers.

Communication Skills
Conflict Management
Creative Thinking
Customer Service
Stress Management
Team Building

Let's look at how Business Coaching has caught on in the business world:

Fortune: "The hottest thing in management today is the executive coach."

Newsweek: "They're part therapist, part consultant—and they sure know how to succeed in business."

Money: "A coach may be the guardian angel you need to rev up your career."

Los Angeles Times: "Boomers find the budding profession can help focus them on business and personal growth"

The Denver Post: "It's tough to develop without help … with coaching you get to see your blind spots in a safe environment."

Executive Female: "Coaching is having a dedicated mentor: it's getting knowledgeable support and encouragement and a new way of looking at things when you need it."

Industry Week: "The benefits of coaching appear to win over even the most cynical clients within just a few weeks."

Appendix 1

Split Screen Experiment:

There is a great experiment that demonstrates this concept called the split screen experiment:

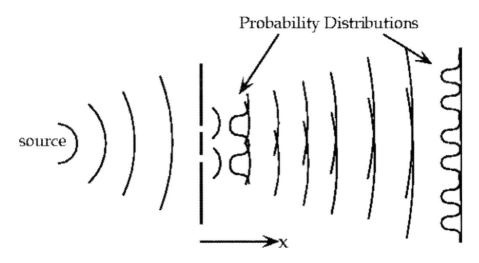

Probability Distributions

Place a gun at the originating point and use a sandbar as the detector. First try covering one slit and see what happens. You get more bullets near the center of the slit and less as you get further away. When you cover the other slit, you see the same thing with respect to the other slit, a particle effect.

In the diagram below, in the center of the experiment is a wall with two slits in it. To the right we have a detector to detect how many electrons we are sending through the experiment reaches each point. To the left of the wall is the originating point of electrons sent through the experiment. The experiment is to send electrons through the two slits and see what happens. Placing an electron gun at the originating point and an electron detector in the detector place.

With the two slits open you get a wavy pattern. The waves reinforced each other creating a larger wave, in other places they cancelled out. In the center is the most overlap. You have seen this effect when two stones are dropped into a lake in different places at the same time; they overlap. The waves each go through both slits, and are able to interfere with themselves. If you want to say that something behaves a certain way or even exists, you must give the context of this behavior or existence since in another context it may behave differently or not exist at all.

Appendix 2

Schrodinger's Cat

Erwin Schrodinger, Physicist 1887 – 1961 Nobel Prize for Physics 1933

Schrodinger devised the cat experiment to illustrate just how radically the quantum realm differs from the macroscopic, everyday world that we inhabit. He himself had shown that a particle such as an electron exists in a number of possible states, the probability of each of which is incorporated into an equation known as the wave function. In the case of an atom of radioactive material, for example, the atom has a certain probability of decaying over a given period of time.

Based on our "classical" intuition, we would assume that there are only two possibilities: either the atom has decayed, or it has not. According to quantum physics, however, the atom inhabits both states simultaneously. It is only when an observer actually tries to determine the state of the atom by measuring it that the wave function "collapses," and the atom assumes just one of its possible states: decayed or not decayed.

Schroedinger reasoned that such probabilistic behavior could exist in the macroscopic world as well, even if we are rarely aware of it. He imagined a box containing an atom having a 50 percent likelihood of decaying in an hour, a radiation detector, a flask containing poison gas and a cat. When or if the atom decays, the Geiger counter will trigger a switch that causes a hammer to smash the flask, releasing the gas and killing the cat. When the experimenter opens the lid of the box and peers inside after an hour has passed, he or she will find the atom either intact or decayed and the cat either alive or dead. But according to quantum mechanics, during the period before the lid is opened, the cat exists in two superposed states: both dead and alive.

Appendix 3

Holographic Image, Karl Pribram

A hologram is a three- dimensional photograph made with the aid of a laser.

To make a hologram, the object to be photographed is first bathed in the light of a laser beam. Then a second laser beam is bounced off the reflected light of the first and the resulting interference pattern (the area where the two laser beams commingle) is captured on film.

When the film is developed, it looks like a meaningless swirl of light and dark lines. But as soon as the developed film is illuminated by another laser beam, a three-dimensional image of the original object appears.

The three-dimensionality of such images is not the only remarkable characteristic of holograms. If a hologram of a rose is cut in half and then illuminated by a laser, each half will still be found to contain the entire image of the rose.

Indeed, even if the halves are divided again, each snippet of film will always be found to contain a smaller but intact version of the original image. Unlike normal photographs, every part of a hologram contains all the information possessed by the whole.

The "whole in every part" nature of a hologram provides us with an entirely new way of understanding organization and order. For most of its history, Western science has labored under the bias that the best way to understand a physical phenomenon, whether a frog or an atom, is to dissect it and study its respective parts.

A hologram teaches us that some things in the universe may not lend themselves to this approach. If we try to take apart something constructed holographic ally, we will not get the pieces of which it is made; we will only get smaller wholes.

Appendix 4

Time Quantized

IS time quantized? In other words, is there a fundamental unit of time that could not be divided into a briefer unit?
Excerpt Courtesy: Jonathan Kent
Brooklyn, NY Scientific American
October 21, 1999

We find that the times involved are always certain special multiples of the 'Planck time,' the shortest time interval consistent with modern physical theories. The model we are working with not only predicts red shifts but also permits a calculation of the mass energies of the basic fundamental particles and of the properties of the fundamental forces. The model implies that time, like space seems to be *three-dimensional*.

We now think that three-dimensional time may be the fundamental matrix of the universe. In this view, fundamental particles and objects—up to the scale of whole galaxies—can be

Deborah Baker-Receniello, PhD, CLSC

represented as discrete quantized structures
of 3-d time embedded within a general matrix
of 3-D time. The structures seem to be
spraying radically outward from an origin
point (time = 0): a big bang in 3-D time. Any
given chunk, say our galaxy, is flowing
outward in 3-D time along its own 1-
dimensional track, a 1-D timeline. Inside our
(quantized) chunk we sense only ordinary 3-D
space, and the single 1-dimension time flow of
our chunk of 3-D time

Appendix 5

Results from Tapes

Some comments in the Medical and Holistic Healing Field from using the audiotapes:

"The soothing, nurturing voice makes you want to embrace the message. Best voice of any guided tape I've heard. The positive messages make these tapes the one's I use and recommend in my Behavior Modification Treatment Plans."

"Recommend these tape to my patients and have found them to be extremely effective. We have tested various tapes with patients. These seem to facilitate more rapid relaxation and recovery. The comments from these patients were very positive in terms of relaxing and helping them manage the pain as well as aiding in their recovery."
Dr. Baker, Oschner Cancer Hospital, New Orleans, La.

"We have found these to serve as anti-depressant in the treatment of substance

abuse. There is a high level of aliveness and relaxation."
George Stephanos, 10 Step Program, Metairie, La.

Some of the professionals researching tapes in their fields:
National Aeronautics and Space Administration (NASA), Gulfport, Ms. – Stress Management

Oschner Clinic, New Orleans, LA - Cancer Patients Community College, Santa Fe, NM - Creativity and Education

Comments by other participants were:

Learning to control energy flow

Learning to control thoughts

Creative energy patterns can be developed with more practice

Increased spiritual and sensory awareness

Feel in control of problems, apply solutions and know I have choices

Increase focus, allows one to be in better touch on ore than one level, very positive experience

Enable me to work at a higher level of productivity

Enjoyed the experience for getting answers—it's simple!

I can affect a healing on my physical body

All subjects responded to relaxation, feeling peacefulness, increased concentration and being in control.

Appendix 6

Thoughts to ponder on love

Here are some thoughts to ponder on love:

Growth is the willingness to let reality be new every moment.
Desires are fulfilled according to your level of awareness
Dreams come true when they are held quietly in the heart
Loving another person is not separate from loving self or God
In duality love comes and goes, in unity there is only love.
Everything is the same spirit watching itself though the eyes of different observers
Others are only mirrors of your own love. In reality there is no other, only Self in other forms.
The outer world contains whispers about the inner world.
Insight is an impulse of love dissolving some old imprint in the brain
Love loves a vacuum

Innocence is the ability to give and receive love without holding on
Innocence is the ability to give and receive love without opposite
Sexual energy is neutral. It can be loving or unloving—it's how you use it
When sex is fully loving, you experience the divine through your partner
To see love in the moment, you must clean the windows of perception

In the moment, there is only love
Love may change, but it never diminishes—it is present

To feel beauty is to know truth. To know the truth is to be in
Love
In the unknown love dances

Appendix 7

Muscle Testing

Muscle Testing allows a convenient communication system or biofeedback loop with the subconscious mind, and when used properly, accurately detect truths. How? The subconscious controls motor functions in the body, like muscle movement, and uses this mechanism to find out when the subconscious agrees or disagrees with a given statement. We use this technique for demonstration and fact-finding is our workshops.

To do this you will need a partner you can trust.

Instructions:

Step 1.   As the person doing the Muscle
           Testing:

   A. Your partner can use either arm for
      testing.   Stand to the side looking over

your partner's shoulder. Have your partner extend the chosen arm.

B. With one hand resting lightly on their extended arm between the wrist and elbow. Place the other hand on their shoulder for stability.

C. Tell your partner to relax, yet keep the arm extended and their chin parallel with the floor, eyes open and focused down. Tell your partner, when you apply pressure on the arm, they are to resist with their arm.

D. Tell your partner to think "strong" just before applying pressure at the wrist. Apply a gentle but steady pressure for about two seconds of until you feel the muscle either lock in place (strong response) or let go, (weak response).

E. Ask your partner if the pressure is comfortable to them. Adjust as you need to and still achieve a clear muscle response.

Step 2.

Muscle Test a statement you know to be TRUE, like (My name is…). Remember to tell your partner "be strong" just before your press gently, so they know when to resist. Note the response.

Then, test a statement you know to be FALSE (My name is a fictitious name). Repeat the above.

NOTE: The response should be STRONG if the statement is TRUE and WEAK if the statement is FALSE. If still unsure of the response, you can practice with different questions like age, occupation, sex, etc). Testing may need practice.

Step 3

If you are comfortable with the Muscle Testing process and your responses, take out the list of beliefs that your partner created previously. Have your partner state the belief. Tell the partner to be strong and apply pressure. If it is a POSITIVE statement, it should test STRONG when the subconscious is in agreement. If the subconscious disagrees, it will test WEAK for a false statement.

Now you have discovered the beliefs that are supported and not supported by your subconscious mind. Usually weak responses will show the lack of support, disappointment, stress, or unfulfilled dreams.

Step 4

After you have tested your beliefs, you now know what changes are necessary. You can begin working on these yourself to create the changes you desire in your life. If you would like assistance in learning about a workshop that teaches you how to create beliefs that support your goals and dreams, rather than sabotage them.

Bibliography

I felt you would appreciate a short list of highly readable books on the major subjects I refer to in this book. All have entered into my own education on these fascinating subjects.

Batie, Howard F., DM, Awakening the Healer Within, Llewellyn Publications 2000

Barnothy, M.F., Biological Effects of Magnet Fields, Vol.2 Plenum Press NY 1969

Backter, Cleve, IANS 1996 The Secret Life of Plants

Baker, Deborah, *Forbidden Crossings*, Blue Star Press, 1995 Poetry

Baker, Deborah, PhD. Effects of REST and Hemispheric Synchronization and Guided Imagery on the Enhancement of Creativity in Problem Solving, Second Annual Conference on REST Journal, New Orleans, LA

Baker, Deborah, PhD. Effects of REST and Sports Performance – Tennis, Third Annual Conference on REST Journal, Santa Fe, New Mexico

Baker, Deborah, PhD, Neuro-Linguistics and Hypnotherapy: A Case Study, Cancer & Stress, Counseling the Cancer Patient, American Journal of Hypnotherapy, New Orleans, LA

Baker, Deborah, PhD, Video entitled: *Subliminals and How the Brain Works,* Webworks, Inc. Television appearance.

Baker, Deborah, PhD, Audio Tapes, *Isn't it about time you used your Whole Brain, 1987.* Developed tapes and trained on utilizing Whole Brain Communication for Stress Reduction, Enhanced Learning, Rewriting a Script, Self Esteem.

Becker, Robert Om M.D. 1985 The Body Electric and Cross Currents

Benor, Daniel J., MD, Spiritual Healing, Vision Publications, 2001

Braden, Gregg, Awakening to Zero Point Any books by this author

Castenados, Carlo, Dreaming, Any Books by this author

Chopra, Deepak, Perfect Health, Quantum Healing, any book by this Author

Cousins, Norman, Anatomy of an Illness, New York: Norton, 1979

Dossey, Larry, M.D. Space, Time, and Medicine. Boston: Shambala, 1982

Femi, Lester, M.D.

Gerber, Richard M.D., Vibrational Medicine, 2001

Haider, Richard, .

Hawkins, David R., MD, Phd, Piower vs Force, 1995, Hay House

Hay, Louise, Heal Your Body, Hay House

Hunt, Valerie, Infinite Mind: The science of human vibrations, 1989: bioenergyfields.org

Hawking, Stephen M., A Brief History of Time, New York: Bantam, 1988

Hooper, Judith and Teresi, Dick, Three Pound Universe

Kaku, Michio, Ph.D. and Jennifer Trainer, Beyond Einstein, New York, Bantam, 1987

Kenyon, Tom, Brain States

Kholodov, Yu: The Effect o Electromagnetic Magnetic Fields on the Central nervous system (1966, NASA - Clearing house for Federal Scientific Technical Information, Springfield, Virginia)
Langer, Ellen, M.D., Mindfulness, 1990

Ledoux, Joseph, Synaptic Self: How our brains become who we are, Viking, 2002

Deborah Baker-Receniello, PhD, CLSC

Mlodinow, Leonard, Euclids Window: Story of Geometry form Parallel Lines to Hyperspace

Myss, Caroline anything by this author

Ornstein, Robert and Thompson Richard, The Amazing Brain

Ornish, Dean, M.D., Any books by this author

Peat, F. David, Philosopher's Stone

Penrose, Roger, Emperor's New Mind

Pert, Candice, Molecules of Emotion

Poe, Richard, Einstein Factor

Pribram, Karl, Holographic Theory

Ramtha's School of Enlightenment, P O Box 519, Yelm, WA 98597 www.ramtha.com For a listing of many books and tapes on consciousness

Ruiz Don Miguel, Sour Agreements, Amber-Allen Publishing, San Rafae, CA 1997

Schrodinger, Erwin, Schrodinger's Cat

Shannahoff-Khalsa, David, Euclid's Window

Simonton, Carl, M.D., Getting Well Again and The Healing Journey, New York: Bantam, 1992

Smitha, Elaine, *If You make the rules How come You're Not Boss*, Webworks Publishing 2003

Steadman, Alice, Who's the Matter With Me?

Talbot, Michael, Holographic Universe

Toben, Bob, Space time and Beyond: Toward an explanation of the Unexplainable New York Dutton, 1982

Wolfe, Fred Alan, Dreaming Universe, 1995, any book by this author

Resources

Services, Exchange, and Renewal in the Olympia, Washington Area

If you have a service you would like to share, email me at:

TakeChargeManifest@hotmail.com

Acupuncture

Alannah Ashlie
Acupuncture & Herbs
Woodinville/Bellvue, WA
425-785-2166, acucolor@hotmail.com
Licensed acupuncturist/color/sound/facial rejuvenation therapist

Deborah Baker-Receniello, PhD, CLSC

Artists

Bobbye Caine
P O Box 1605
Yelm, WA 98597
360 458 5732 mindsx7@yahoo.com

Joyous Creations
Robin Lee
P O Box 1188
Rainier, WA 98576
360 446 1619 www.joyouscreations.com

Attorney

Jessica McKeegan Jensen, Esq.
Jessica McKeegan Jensen, PC
6245 Guerin Street SW
Olympia, WA 98512-2244
lexlux@earthlink.net phone 360-352-7965
fax 360-570-2038

Coaching

Deborah Baker-Receniello, PhD, CLSC,
DBR Life & Business Coach, Inc.
PMB 209 800 Sleater Kinney SE
Lacey, WA 98501 email: dbrcoaching@comcast.net
Web: www.dbrlifecoach.com

Chiropractic

Rainier Chiropractic Clinic
P O Box 656 - 109 Binghamton St E. Ste D
Rainier, WA 98576
360 446 3151 fax: 360 446 310
Dr. Joe Dispensa
Dr. Bill Harrell

Consulting Services

Marge Mohoric, Ph.D., Partner
The Paragon Consulting Group
Olympia, WA
Toll free: 888.755.2725 x105
mmohoric@theparagongroup.com

Editor/Consultant/Manuscript Preparation

Bev Stumf
Editor, Writer, Consultant
1420 NW Gilman Blvd # 2835
Issaquah, WA 98027-7001 bwrite@attbi.com

Energy Work & Reiki

Howard F. Batie, Mh.D., Director
Evergreen Healing Arts Center
1570 N National Ave, Ste 102
Chehalis, Washington
www.localaccess.com/HealingHands 360 748 7287

Deborah Baker-Receniello, PhD, CLSC

Susan Leland, Energy Healing Practitioner
1001 Cooper Point Rd SW, Suite 140-140, Olympia, WA 98502
360-754-2350
Email: revsacredforest@aol.com

Ely Leduc, RN
Healing Touch, Shamanism Healing
The Mars ton Center
677 Woodland Square Loop SW
Lacey, WA 98503 360 438-1244 cell 360 280-1083
elly@babymassage.net www.themarstoncenter.com

Fashion Design

Flo Thomas
Owner/Independent Fashion Coordinator
Weekenders USA
606 Lilly Road NE #621
Olympia 98506
360 456-6810 flothomas@reachone.com

Herbal Astrography

Isa 'Kitty' Mady,
Roseworks Botanicals, (360) 249-5364
Herbal Astrography Readings & Classes - The combined use of herbs, astrology & graphology (penmanship) for developing awareness & creating change.

Home Mortgage/Loans

Wells Fargo Home Mortgage
4200 6th Avenue SE, Suite 205
Lacey, WA 98503
Email lee.hauser@wellsfargo.com
Tara Hall, Source Financial
P O Box 2111
Yelm, WA 98597
360 458 8455 fax 360 458 2461

Lee A. Hauser
Home Mortgage Consultant
Office 360-486-3659
Toll Free 800-876-1160, Extension 1012
Fax 360-486-0978 Cell 360-791-9763

HYPNOTHERAPY

Transformations
3131 Sapp Rd SW, Tumwater, WA 98512
360 754-1024
emails: Transformation_Hypno@NetZero.net

Massage

Sandi McCarthy
Massage & 'Aqua Chi'™ Machine Therapy
Phone: 360 866 9634

Jalene Smith
Massage & Colon Hydrotherapy
Phone: 866 9634

Deborah Baker-Receniello, PhD, CLSC

Sandra Lynn Lee
LMP, SOMA
515 State Ave
Olympia, WA 360 943 1946

Organizations

South Puget Sound Wellness Association
PSWA is dedicated to unifying people through wellness, research, education and community service
Email: info@pugetsoundwellness.com website: www.pugetsoundwellness.com

Professional Connections for Women
Monthly Connections breakfast meeting
360 456-4486 email: plakos@orcalink.com

Public Accountants

Kim Adney, EA
Siminski & Associates, PS
1411 State Ave NE, Suite 200
Olympia, WA 98506
(360) 956-1040 phone (360) 956-9896 fax
ka@siminski.com

Reflexology

Terralynn Hoskins, Director
International School of Reflexology & Meridian Therapy
P O Box 14724
Tumwater, WA 98511
www.isrmtusa.com Email: isrmtusa@comcast.net

Resumes

Colleen Kemp
Creative Résumés
1017 4th Avenue East
Olympia, WA 98506
(360) 352-1057 www.creativeresumes.net
Email: ckemp1@qwest.net

Television Host/Producer

Elaine Smitha
Television host/producer - *Evolving Ideas*
www.elainesmitha.com
Webworks Publishing, PO Box 3695, Olympia, WA 98509
Phone: 360-491-3714 Fax: 360-491-6732
publishing@evolvingideas.com

Web Hosting, Computer Support

Prairie Techies
Michael Armstrong
www.prairietechies.com
360 894 1779 michelle@prairietechies.com

Weblink Visions, Inc.
Linking your visions to the web and beyond
www.weblinkvisions.com

During a meditation I asked my Spirit to reveal itself to me through an experience. The meditation lasted for an hour and a half.

Deborah Baker-Receniello, PhD, CLSC

If I wrote that it would take many pages.
Here's a poem that came out of it.

>I sing my song of growth
>Within the sap of every plant
>I touch every fish, every bird
>Every creature of water, land or air
>
>I am the carrier of life in
>Everything on the planet and beyond
>It is I that triggers
>Vitality and life in every seed
>
>All life bows in respect
>Homage paid is love
>I combine with and radiate forth
>The creative power of unconditional love
>
>I chant to the dolphins of the
>Oneness of all life
>As I tone, I evoke that which
>Uplifts and honors all of life
>
>I as Spirit create this body
>For pure expression
>I am not the body
>I am that which permeates and animates
>
>I resonate to the soul you see
>Never to the human mind or id
>Surrounded by abundant life
>Of a multidimensional reality

Deborah Baker-Receniello

Deborah Baker-Receniello, Ph.D., CLSC
Olympia, WA
Email: TakeChargeManifest.hotmail.com

About the Author

A resourceful and creative problem-solver with the ability to cut to the heart of a matter, gather proper resources and achieve positive results. A take-charge professional who has worked closely with top-management and teams with extensive experience in branch management, public service, communication, training, counseling and marketing. I am creative, with an orderly mind and can write clear, concise information. I am a member of the Society of Children's Book Writers and Illustrators, Pacific Northwest Writers, Writer4Kids and a graduate of Children's Writers Boot Camp. Presently: a Certified Life

Strategies and Business Coach, facilitator, author and speaker.

Advanced Degrees: Business Administration and Counseling Psychology

Certification: Life Strategies and Business Coach

Board of Directors: *The Oakville Cruiser*
Founder: Puget Sound Wellness Association

Non-Fiction
Grant Writing: Successfully wrote grant for Oakville Children's Garden, 1997 ($2,500)
Grant for Research and Development, along with Training, Major Fortune Company 1985 ($150,000)

Business Writing: Brochures, Newsletters, Publication, Promotion pieces (Word, Excel, Publisher, Power Point) presently learning Page Maker, Photoshop and Adobe

Published Articles:
Monthly column, *Library Highlights*, for the *Oakville Cruiser*, Oakville, WA 1995-Present

Human Interest Articles and Poetry for the *Oakville Cruiser*, Oakville, WA 1995-Present

Effects of REST and Hemispheric Synchronization and Guided Imagery on the Enhancement of Creativity in Problem Solving, Second Annual Conference on REST Journal, New Orleans, LA

Effects of REST and Sports Performance - Tennis, Third Annual Conference on REST Journal, Santa Fe, New Mexico

Neuro-Linguistics and Hypnotherapy: A Case Study, Cancer & Stress, Counseling the Cancer Patient, American Journal of Hypnotherapy, New Orleans, LA

Development, Training and Public Speaking:

Lifestyle Education for Wellness, Developed workbook and training program approved by the Academy of Clinical Hypnosis and American Association of Nurse Anesthetists, New Orleans, LA.

Developed four Audio Cassette Tape Album, *Pemsystems, Isn't it about time you used your WholeBrain.* Developed tapes and trained on utilizing Whole Brain Communication for Stress Reduction, Enhanced Learning, Rewriting a Script, Self Esteem.

Video, *Subliminals and How the Brain Works,* Webworks, Inc. Television appearance.

Various Seminars: Developed and presented many seminars in Whole Brain Communications, Learning Styles, Sales, Motivation and Poetry.

Young Authors Workshop, Poetry Workshop Leader, Aberdeen, WA 1995

Fiction

Awards:

Rainbow Ribbon, Famous Poets Society, Winner of the Diamond Homer Trophy and inducted into the International Poetry Hall of Fame, 1995

The Traveler, Winner- Honorable Mention, Iliad Press, Troy, MI

In the Night, President's Award, Excellence, Iliad Press

Summer's Day, Honorable Mention, *International Poets Society*

Who's Who in Human Service Professionals, 1988

Poetry Published in following Anthologies:

In the Night, A Voyage to Remember Anthology, National Library of Poetry, Owings, MA
What Do You See, Poetic Voices of America, Sparrowgrass Poetry Forum
Rainbow Ribbon, Today's Great Poems, Famous Poet's Society, Hollywood, CA
Transformation, National Library of Poetry
Where Did You Come From? ISSAC Forum
In the Night, Iliad Press
Reflections of Midnight Blue, Isle of View Anthology, National Library of Poetry
Unseen, Nature's Echoes Anthology, National Library of Poetry
The Traveler, Iliad Press
Truth Unseen, Letters from the Soul, *www.Poetry.com, Owings Mills, MD*
Summer's Day, International Poets Society, Oregon

Research Quoted

New Tools and Techniques for Brain Growth and Mind Expansion, MEGABRAIN, by Michael Hutchinson

Published Books:

Forbidden Crossings, Blue Star Press, Oakville, WA Poetry and Prose 1995

A Writing Sampler, Davis Creek Farm, Oakville, WA Poetry and Children's Stories 1993

Why It Works: The Science Behind Manifesting Everything You Desire, AuthorHouse.com 2004

Printed in the United States
69581LVS00005B/148-150

9 781418 447403